Teen Smoking

Other Books of Related Interest:

Opposing Viewpoints Series

America's Youth

Teen Drug Abuse

Current Controversies

Drug Trafficking

At Issue Series

Heroin

Perfomance-Enhancing Drugs

CONTEMPORARY
ISSUES
COMPANION

Teen Smoking

Stefan Kiesbye, Book Editor

GREENHAVEN PRESS

An imprint of Thomson Gale, a part of The Thomson Corporation

THOMSON

GALE

Detroit • New York • San Francisco • New Haven, Conn. • Waterville, Maine • London

Christine Nasso, *Publisher*
Elizabeth Des Chenes, *Managing Editor*

© 2008 The Gale Group.

Star logo is a trademark and Gale and Greenhaven Press are registered trademarks used herein under license.

For more information, contact:
Greenhaven Press
27500 Drake Rd.
Farmington Hills, MI 48331-3535
Or you can visit our Internet site at http://www.gale.com

ISBN-13: 978-0-7377-2464-6 (hardcover)
ISBN-10: 0-7377-2464-1 (hardcover)
ISBN-13: 978-0-7377-2465-3 (pbk.)
ISBN-10: 0-7377-2465-X (pbk.)

Library of Congress Control Number: 2007938431

Contents

Foreword

In the news, on the streets, and in neighborhoods, individuals are confronted with a variety of social problems. Such problems may affect people directly: A young woman may struggle with depression, suspect a friend of having bulimia, or watch a loved one battle cancer. And even the issues that do not directly affect her private life—such as religious cults, domestic violence, or legalized gambling—still impact the larger society in which she lives. Discovering and analyzing the complexities of issues that encompass communal and societal realms as well as the world of personal experience is a valuable educational goal in the modern world.

Effectively addressing social problems requires familiarity with a constantly changing stream of data. Becoming well informed about today's controversies is an intricate process that often involves reading myriad primary and secondary sources, analyzing political debates, weighing various experts' opinions—even listening to firsthand accounts of those directly affected by the issue. For students and general observers, this can be a daunting task because of the sheer volume of information available in books, periodicals, on the evening news, and on the Internet. Researching the consequences of legalized gambling, for example, might entail sifting through congressional testimony on gambling's societal effects, examining private studies on Indian gaming, perusing numerous Web sites devoted to Internet betting, and reading essays written by lottery winners as well as interviews with recovering compulsive gamblers. Obtaining valuable information can be time-consuming—since it often requires researchers to pore over numerous documents and commentaries before discovering a source relevant to their particular investigation.

Greenhaven's Contemporary Issues Companion series seeks to assist this process of research by providing readers with useful and pertinent information about today's complex issues. Each volume in this anthology series focuses on a topic of current interest, presenting informative and thought-provoking selections written from a wide variety of viewpoints. The readings selected by the editors include such diverse sources as personal accounts and case studies, pertinent factual and statistical articles, and relevant commentaries and overviews. This diversity of sources and views, found in every Contemporary Issues Companion, offers readers a broad perspective in one convenient volume.

In addition, each title in the Contemporary Issues Companion series is designed especially for young adults. The selections included in every volume are chosen for their accessibility and are expertly edited in consideration of both the reading and comprehension levels of the audience. The structure of the anthologies also enhances accessibility. An introductory essay places each issue in context and provides helpful facts such as historical background or current statistics and legislation that pertain to the topic. The chapters that follow organize the material and focus on specific aspects of the book's topic. Every essay is introduced by a brief summary of its main points and biographical information about the author. These summaries aid in comprehension and can also serve to direct readers to material of immediate interest and need. Finally, a comprehensive index allows readers to efficiently scan and locate content.

The Contemporary Issues Companion series is an ideal launching point for research on a particular topic. Each anthology in the series is composed of readings taken from an extensive gamut of resources, including periodicals, newspapers, books, government documents, the publications of private and public organizations, and Internet Web sites. In these volumes, readers will find factual support suitable for use in reports, debates, speeches, and research papers. The anthologies also facilitate further research, featuring a book and periodical bibliography and a list of organizations to contact for additional information.

A perfect resource for both students and the general reader, Greenhaven's Contemporary Issues Companion series is sure to be a valued source of current, readable information on social problems that interest young adults. It is the editors' hope that readers will find the Contemporary Issues Companion series useful as a starting point to formulate their own opinions about and answers to the complex issues of the present day.

Introduction

Smoking is a hazardous and potentially harmful habit. No one, not even the tobacco industry, denies this anymore. Yet smoking also has a long history, and is often associated with peace, calm, cool, and style. Ever since the birth of movies, smoking has been a choice activity for action heroes and party animals, for cops and gangsters alike. It is hard to imagine a young Audrey Hepburn without a cigarette holder, or to see Bruce Willis dying hard without a lighter. Femininity and sexual suggestiveness, as well as masculinity, have always been linked with the use of tobacco.

Smoking is a cultural activity as much as a physical one. Like alcohol and coffee, cigarettes do not fulfill basic needs. The Web site KidsHealth declares, "There are no physical reasons to *start* smoking—the body doesn't need tobacco the way it needs food, water, sleep, and exercise. In fact, many of the chemicals in cigarettes, like nicotine and cyanide, are actually poisons that can kill in high enough doses. The body's smart and it goes on the defense when it's being poisoned. For this reason, many people find it takes several tries to get started smoking: First-time smokers often feel pain or burning in the throat and lungs, and some people feel sick or even throw up the first few times they try tobacco." Tobacco then, is not about consumption, but about identity. The product has the capability of defining who the consumer is.

Film, advertising, and magazines have been portraying smoking as a glamorous activity for so long that the use of tobacco has become synonymous with cool. Not surprisingly then, the majority of smokers take up the habit as teenagers. It is a way to look older, look trendy, impress peers, or just to follow the lead of the cool kids. Yet it is a hard habit to kick, even when the smoker has outgrown the need for looking cool. Smoking is addictive, and what might start as gesturing has the potential of causing serious illness later in life.

The public concern for underage smokers might be part of the reason why Big Tobacco—a pejorative term for the lucrative tobacco industry—has been under attack for a number of years now. As the American Academy of Family Physicians states, "Cigarettes contain disgusting things that you would never think about putting in your body. For example, cigarettes contain tar, carbon monoxide, chemicals like DDT, arsenic and formaldehyde (a gas used to preserve dead animals). The tobacco in cigarettes also contains nicotine—the drug that makes smoking addictive. All of these things are bad for your body. Nicotine raises your risk of heart attack and stroke. Tar and carbon monoxide cause serious breathing problems. And . . . tobacco smoke causes cancer." These are alarming facts. In addition, it is easy to drink your cappuccino or wine without bothering anyone sitting at your table or beyond, but impossible when smoking a cigarette. Secondhand smoke, which some scientists claim can be very harmful, has padded the case of antismoking campaigns against tobacco. The American Lung association writes, "Secondhand smoke causes about 3,000 deaths each year from lung cancer in nonsmokers," and "Secondhand smoke has been estimated to cause 22,700–69,600 deaths per year from heart disease in adult nonsmokers."

Yet recently, the attackers have come under attack as well. Researchers and beleaguered smokers have stated that the statistics widely used to prove the dangers of smoking are exaggerated and based on "junk" science. They are not denying that cigarettes are detrimental to one's health, but point out that so is eating sugar and deep-fried foods, drinking coffee, driving a motorcycle or car, or running road races. And while it is true that teenagers are impressionable and in danger of starting an unhealthy and lifelong habit, the same can be said for alcohol, coffee, driving, and any number of questionable activities, smoking proponents assert. Smoking is a legal activity—unless you light up a pipe or cigarette in places where it is specifically banned—so why do we see large-scale campaigns against it, but not against sugary drinks, sweet treats, or driving?

Writer Olavo de Carvalho, commenting on antismoking campaigns, muses, "People who believe themselves to be passive smokers are gently invited to avoid my company. I rather believe [in] Santa Claus than the effects of passive smoking. Even of active smoking. You know, I am an impressionable guy. The other day my beloved aunt Paula died. She worked to the last day and she smoked cigarettes to the last minute. The doctors said cigarettes killed her. The poor lady was only 91 years old."

Entering the ongoing debate requires research and an open mind. Is smoking worse than eating cupcakes? Who is affected by Big Tobacco's ad campaigns? Is tobacco a drug, or is it a luxury article on par with a mocha? Who has the say in banning smoking, and are these bans necessary and successful? Do antismoking campaigns reach the teenagers they are intended for, or do they have the opposite effect and convince young people that smoking is desirable, since forbidden?

Every serious discussion of smoking has to include the cultural implications. Tobacco has been with us since the dawn of humankind. In ancient Egypt, in medieval Europe, and in the native cultures of the Americas, smoking was a civilized and highly ritualized activity. In order to ban smoking or even erase it, we would have to reevaluate our attitudes toward nutrition, to leisure, and toward the images of ourselves.

A picture of the young Clint Eastwood with a cigarette dangling from the corner of his mouth says more than any lecture by parents and teachers. Smoking gangsters in *Reservoir Dogs* might be more convincing than TV commercials against tobacco use. And who is right—those who speak out against tobacco use, or those people who believe that the dangers of smoking have been overstated? It is an ongoing battle between those who feel that we can eradicate one of the biggest health issues if we try hard enough, and those who see the fight against smoking as a new form of prohibition. If we want to take sides, we have the responsibility to choose wisely.

CHAPTER 1

Teen Tobacco Use and the War on Smoking

Child and Teen Tobacco Use

Scholastic

It is well established that tobacco addiction is a deadly habit. In the following viewpoint Scholastic presents research results and information about the dangers of tobacco addiction and second-hand smoke. The article also addresses the issue of teens and tobacco use, arguing that teens who use tobacco are more likely than adults to become addicted. Scholastic is a publisher and distributor of children's books, a creator of magazines, software, and television shows, and a leader in e-commerce and educational technology.

Tobacco is one of the most heavily used addictive products in the United States, according to the National Institute on Drug Abuse (NIDA). In 2004, 70.3 million people used tobacco at least once in the month before being interviewed. That is more than 25 percent of the U.S. population 12 and older.

Nicotine is the main ingredient in tobacco that causes addiction. Research shows that nicotine activates the parts of the brain that control feelings of pleasure. Nicotine works fast. Drug levels peak within 10 seconds of inhalation. (Cigar and pipe smokers and smokeless tobacco users absorb nicotine more slowly.) Within a few minutes, the effects of nicotine disappear. To keep feeling good, a smoker takes another puff or lights another cigarette.

Smoking harms every organ in the body. Cigarette smoking accounts for about one-third of all cancer deaths, including those from lung cancer. In fact, cigarette smoking has been linked to about 90 percent of all lung cancer cases. Research shows that smoking increases the risk of heart disease. Smokers harm others as well as themselves through secondhand smoke.

Teens and Tobacco

The Facts According to the Monitoring the Future Survey for 2005, cigarette smoking among students is at the lowest levels in the history of the survey. Since 1975 the survey has measured drug, alcohol, cigarette use, and related attitudes among students in 8th, 10th, and 12th grades nationwide. This decrease in use corresponds to a continuous increase in the number of teens who believe there are "great" health risks from cigarette smoking.

While this is good news, research suggests that teens who do use tobacco are more likely than adults to become addicted. Even occasional smoking can result in tobacco addiction in some teens. In animal research, investigators have shown adolescents to be more susceptible to the effects of nicotine than adults. (For more about teen health dangers, see Latest Research, below.)

Secondhand Smoke: A Real Danger

Cigarette smoke contains thousands of dangerous chemicals that are unhealthy for both smokers and nonsmokers. Secondhand smoke refers to the smoke from the burning end of a cigarette and the smoke exhaled by smokers. More than 126 million Americans are regularly exposed to secondhand smoke at home, at work, and in enclosed public spaces.

The Deadly Effects

Secondhand smoke can cause heart disease and lung cancer in nonsmoking adults. Breathing secondhand smoke for even a short time increases risk for those diseases.

Children and infants are especially vulnerable to the poisons in secondhand smoke. Almost 3 million children in the

United States under the age of six breathe secondhand smoke at home at least four days per week.

Secondhand smoke is a known cause of sudden infant death syndrome (SIDS), respiratory problems, ear infections, and asthma attacks in infants and children.

Secondhand smoke in the home environment can slow the lung growth of exposed children. Older children whose parents smoke get bronchitis and pneumonia more often than the children of nonsmokers.

Wheezing and coughing are also more common in children who breathe secondhand smoke.

Protecting Yourself and Others

The only way to fully protect yourself and loved ones from the dangerous chemicals in secondhand smoke is through 100 percent smoke-free environments. Opening a window; sitting in a separate area; or using ventilation, air conditioning, or a fan cannot eliminate secondhand smoke exposure. If you are a smoker, the single best way to protect your family is to quit smoking.

Latest Research

Addiction is a developmental disorder that begins in adolescence, and sometimes as early as childhood. Recent advances have provided more insight into why teens put themselves at risk for addiction through risk-taking and thrill-seeking behaviors. These behaviors are likely due to the fact that the part of the brain responsible for judgment, decision making, and control of emotional responses—the prefrontal cortex—is the last area of the brain to mature. But there may be other factors.

Dr. James Belluzzi and colleagues have recently found that a chemical in tobacco smoke, acetaldehyde, may play a role in addicting adolescents to smoking. In the study, adolescent laboratory rats increased their intake of nicotine when it was combined with acetaldehyde. Adult rats did not.

All the rats were placed in cages where they could poke their noses through holes and receive either nicotine, saline, acetaldehyde, or a mixture of acetaldehyde and nicotine.

Over five days, with increasing frequency, the adolescent rats showed a preference for the acetaldehyde-nicotine combination. The adult rats did not show any preference.

"Our results show that acetaldehyde, at the same relative concentration found in cigarette smoke, dramatically increases the reinforcing properties of nicotine," says Dr. Belluzzi. "Furthermore, the effect is age-related, with adolescent animals far more sensitive than adults."

Overcoming Tobacco Addiction

Quitting Has Immediate Health Benefits Within 24 hours of quitting, blood pressure goes down and chances of heart attack decrease. Long-term benefits of quitting include lower risk of stroke, lung and other cancers, and coronary heart disease.

Treating Withdrawal from Nicotine

- Nicotine withdrawal symptoms include irritability, craving, cognitive and attention deficits, sleep disturbances, and increased appetite.

- To reduce the symptoms, nicotine replacements—gum, patches, sprays, and inhalers—are used. Another medication works on other areas of the brain to control craving.

- Newer medications under study act on nicotine receptors directly. Studies show that medications have better long-term success when combined with behavioral treatment.

Lies About Smoking and Secondhand Smoke

Robert A. Levy and Rosalind B. Marimont

The same statistics about the dangers of smoking appear again and again, in a plethora of articles, on numerous Web sites, and in many health brochures. But where do they come from and are they true? In this article, Robert Levy and Rosalind Marimont take a critical view of the anti-tobacco campaign and of the numbers that have been widely circulated. Especially the evidence against secondhand smoke, they claim, is too thin to be believed. They conclude that politics have obliterated sound science and judgment. Levy is a Cato Institute senior fellow and an adjunct professor at Georgetown University Law Center; Marimont is retired from the U.S. National Institute of Standards and Technology and the National Institutes of Health.

Truth was an early victim in the battle against tobacco. The big lie, repeated ad nauseam in anti-tobacco circles, is that smoking causes more than 400,000 premature deaths each year in the United States. That mantra is the principal justification for all manner of tobacco regulations and legislation, not to mention lawsuits by dozens of states for Medicaid recovery, class actions by seventy-five to eighty union health funds, similar litigation by thirty-five Blue Cross plans, twenty-four class suits by smokers who are not yet ill, sixty class actions by allegedly ill smokers, five hundred suits for damages from secondhand smoke, and health-related litigation by twelve cities and counties—an explosion of adjudication never before experienced in this country or elsewhere.

The war on smoking started with a kernel of truth—that cigarettes are a high risk factor for lung cancer—but has grown

Robert A. Levy and Rosalind B. Marimont, "Lies, Damned Lies, & 400,000 Smoking-Related Deaths," *Regulation*, vol. 21, 1998, pp. 24–29.

into a monster of deceit and greed, eroding the credibility of government and subverting the rule of law. Junk science has replaced honest science and propaganda parades as fact. Our legislators and judges, in need of dispassionate analysis, are instead smothered by an avalanche of statistics—tendentious, inadequately documented, and unchecked by even rudimentary notions of objectivity. Meanwhile, Americans are indoctrinated by health "professionals" bent on imposing their lifestyle choices on the rest of us and brainwashed by politicians eager to tap the deep pockets of a pariah industry. . . .

Third-Rate Thinking About Secondhand Smoke

"Passive Smoking Does Cause Lung Cancer, Do Not Let Them Fool You," states the headline of a March 1998 press release from the World Health Organization [WHO]. The release begins by noting that WHO had been accused of suppressing its own study because it "failed to scientifically prove that there is an association between passive smoking . . . and a number of diseases, lung cancer in particular." Not true, insisted WHO. Smokers themselves are not the only ones who suffer health problems because of their habit. Secondhand smoke can be fatal as well.

The press release went on to report that WHO researchers found "an estimated 16 percent increased risk of lung cancer among nonsmoking spouses of smokers. For workplace exposure the estimated increase in risk was 17 percent." Remarkably, the very next line warned: "Due to small sample size, neither increased risk was statistically significant." Contrast that conclusion with the hype in the headline: "Passive Smoking Does Cause Lung Cancer." Spoken often enough, the lie becomes its own evidence.

Results Were Misinterpreted

The full study would not see the light of day for seven more months, until October 1998, when it was finally published in the *Journal of the National Cancer Institute*. News reports omitted any mention of statistical insignificance. Instead, they again trumpeted relative risks of 1.16 and 1.17, corresponding to 16 and 17 percent increases, as if those ratios were meaningful. Somehow lost in WHO's media blitz was the National Cancer Institute's own guideline: "Relative risks of less than 2 [that is, a 100 percent increase] are considered small. . . . Such increases may be due to chance, statistical bias, or effects of confounding factors that are sometimes not evident." To put the WHO results in their proper perspective, note that the relative risk of lung cancer for persons who drink whole milk is 2.4. That is, the increased risk of contracting lung cancer from whole milk is 140 percent—more than eight times the 17 percent increase from secondhand smoke.

What should have mattered most to government officials, the health community and concerned parents is the following pronouncement from the WHO study: After examining 650 lung cancer patients and 1,500 healthy adults in seven European countries, WHO concluded that the "results indicate no association between childhood exposure to environmental tobacco smoke and lung cancer risk."

EPA Junk Science

Another example of anti-tobacco misinformation is the landmark 1993 report in which the Environmental Protection Agency declared that environmental tobacco smoke (ETS) is a dangerous carcinogen that kills three thousand Americans yearly. Five years later, in July 1998, federal judge William L. Osteen lambasted the EPA for "cherry picking" the data, excluding studies that "demonstrated no association between ETS and cancer," and withholding "significant portions of its findings and reasoning in striving to confirm its *a priori* hypothesis." Both "the record and EPA's explanation," concluded the court, "make it clear that using standard methodology,

EPA could not produce statistically significant results." A more damning assessment is difficult to imagine. . . .

Hysteria Replaced People's Judgment

Hundreds of states, cities, and counties have banned indoor smoking—many in reaction to the EPA report. California even prohibits smoking in bars. According to Matthew L. Myers, general counsel of the Campaign for Tobacco-Free Kids, "the release of the original risk assessment gave an enormous boost to efforts to restrict smoking." Now that the study has been thoroughly debunked, one would think that many of the bans would be lifted. Don't hold your breath. When science is adulterated and debased for political ends, the culprits are unlikely to reverse course merely because they have been unmasked.

In reaction to the federal court's criticism EPA administrator Carol M. Browner said, "It's so widely accepted that secondhand smoke causes very real problems for kids and adults. Protecting people from the health hazards of secondhand smoke should be a national imperative." Like *Alice in Wonderland*, sentence first, evidence afterward. Browner reiterates: "We believe the health threats . . . from breathing secondhand smoke are very real." Never mind science; it is Browner's beliefs that control. The research can be suitably tailored.

For the EPA to alter results, disregard evidence, and adjust its procedures and standards to satisfy agency prejudices is unacceptable behavior, even to a first-year science student. Those criticisms are about honesty, carefulness, and rigor— the very essence of science.

Classifying Diseases as Smoking-Related

With that record of distortion, it should come as no surprise that anti-tobacco crusaders misrepresent the number of deaths due to smoking. Start by considering the diseases that are incorrectly classified as smoking-related. The Centers for Disease

Control and Prevention (CDC) prepares and distributes information on smoking-attributable mortality, morbidity and economic costs (SAMMEC). In its *Morbidity and Mortality Weekly Report* for 27 August 1993, the CDC states that 418,690 Americans died in 1990 of various diseases that they contracted because, according to the government, they smoked.

Diseases are categorized as smoking-related if the risk of death for smokers exceeds that for nonsmokers. In the jargon of epidemiology, a relative risk that is greater than 1 indicates a connection between exposure (smoking) and effect (death). Recall, however, the National Cancer Institute's guideline: "Relative risks of less than two are considered small. . . . Such increases may be due to chance, statistical bias, or effects of confounding factors that are sometimes not evident." And the *Federal Reference Manual on Scientific Evidence* confirms that the threshold test for legal significance is a relative risk of two or higher. At any ratio below two, the results are insufficiently reliable to conclude that a particular agent (e.g., tobacco) caused a particular disease.

What would happen if the SAMMEC data were to exclude deaths from those diseases that had a relative risk of less than two for current or former smokers? . . . 163,071 deaths reported by CDC were from diseases that should not have been included in the report. Add to that another 1,362 deaths from burn injuries—unless one believes that Philip Morris is responsible when a smoker falls asleep with a lit cigarette. That is a total of 164,433 misreported deaths out of 418,690. When the report is properly limited to diseases that have a significant relationship with smoking, the death total declines to 254,257. Thus, on this count alone, SAMMEC overstates the number of deaths by 65 percent.

Calculating Excess Deaths

But there is more. Writing on "Risk Attribution and Tobacco-Related Deaths" in the 1993 *American Journal of Epidemiology*,

T.D. Sterling, W.L. Rosenbaum, and J.J. Weinkam expose another overstatement—exceeding 65 percent—that flows from using the American Cancer Society's Cancer Prevention Survey (CPS) as a baseline against which excess deaths are computed. Here is how one government agency, the Office of Technology Assessment (OTA), calculates the number of deaths caused by smoking:

The OTA first determines the death rate for persons who were part of the CPS sample and never smoked. Next, that rate is applied to the total U.S. population in order to estimate the number of Americans who would have died if no one ever smoked. Finally, the hypothetical number of deaths for assumed never-smokers is subtracted from the actual number of U.S. deaths, and the difference is ascribed to smoking. That approach seems reasonable if one important condition is satisfied: The CPS sample must be roughly the same as the overall U.S. population with respect to those factors, other than smoking, that could be associated with the death rate. But as Sterling, Rosenbaum, and Weinkam point out, nothing could be further from the truth.

The American Cancer Society bases its CPS study on a million men and women volunteers, drawn from the ranks of the Society's members, friends, and acquaintances. The persons who participate are more affluent than average, overwhelmingly white, married, college graduates, who generally do not have hazardous jobs. Each of those characteristics tends to reduce the death rate of the CPS sample which, as a result, enjoys an average life expectancy that is substantially longer than the typical American enjoys.

Biased Science

Because OTA starts with an atypically low death rate for never-smokers in the CPS sample, then applies that rate to the whole population, its baseline for determining excess deaths is grossly underestimated. By comparing actual deaths with a baseline that is far too low, OTA creates the illusion that a large number of deaths are due to smoking.

That same illusion pervades the statistics released by the U.S. Surgeon General, who in his 1989 report estimated that 335,600 deaths were caused by smoking. When Sterling, Rosenbaum, and Weinkam recalculated the Surgeon General's numbers, replacing the distorted CPS sample with a more representative baseline from large surveys conducted by the National Center for Health Statistics, they found that the number of smoking-related deaths declined to 203,200. Thus, the Surgeon General's report overstated the number of deaths by more than 65 percent simply by choosing the wrong standard of comparison.

Sterling and his coauthors report that not only is the death rate considerably lower for the CPS sample than for the entire U.S. but, astonishingly, even smokers in the CPS sample have a lower death rate than the national average for both smokers and nonsmokers. As a result, if OTA were to have used the CPS death rate for smokers, applied that rate to the total population, then subtracted the actual number of deaths for all Americans, it would have found that smoking saves 277,621 lives each year. The authors caution, of course, that their calculation is sheer nonsense, not a medical miracle. Those "lives would be saved only if the U.S. population would die with the death rate of smokers in the affluent CPS sample."

Unhappily, the death rate for Americans is considerably higher than that for the CPS sample. Nearly as disturbing, researchers like Sterling, Rosenbaum, and Weinkam identified that statistical predicament many years ago; yet the government persists in publishing data on smoking-related deaths that are known to be greatly inflated.

Controlling for Confounding Variables

Even if actual deaths were compared against an appropriate baseline for nonsmokers, the excess deaths could not properly be attributed to smoking alone. It cannot be assumed that the only difference between smokers and nonsmokers is that the former smoke. The two groups are dissimilar in many other respects, some of which affect their propensity to contract diseases that have been identified as smoking-related. For instance, smokers have higher rates of alcoholism, exercise less on average, eat fewer green vegetables, are more likely to be exposed to workplace carcinogens, and are poorer than nonsmokers. Each of those factors can be a "cause" of death from a so-called smoking-related disease; and each must be statistically controlled for if the impact of a single factor, like smoking, is to be reliably determined.

Sterling, Rosenbaum, and Weinkam found that adjusting their calculations for just two lifestyle differences—in income and alcohol consumption—between smokers and nonsmokers had the effect of reducing the Surgeon General's smoking-related death count still further, from 203,200 to 150,000. That means the combined effect of using a proper standard of comparison coupled with controls for income and alcohol was to lower the Surgeon General's estimate 55 percent—from 335,600 to 150,000. Thus, the original estimate was a disquieting 124 percent too high, even without adjustments for important variables like occupation, exercise, and nutritional habits.

What if smokers got plenty of exercise and had healthy diets while nonsmokers were couch potatoes who consumed buckets of fast food? Naturally, there are some smokers and nonsmokers who satisfy those criteria. Dr. William E. Wecker, a consulting statistician who has testified for the tobacco industry, scanned the CPS database and found thousands of smokers with relatively low risk factors and thousands of never-smokers with high risk factors. Comparing the mortality rates of the two groups, Dr. Wecker discovered that the smokers were "healthier and die less often by a factor of three than the never-smokers." Obviously, other risk factors matter, and any study that ignores them is utterly worthless.

Yet, if a smoker who is obese; has a family history of high cholesterol, diabetes, and heart problems; and never exercises dies of a heart attack, the government attributes his death to smoking alone. That procedure, if applied to the other causal factors identified in the CPS study, would produce more than twice as many "attributed" deaths as there are actual deaths, according to Dr. Wecker. For example, the same calculations that yield 400,000 smoking-related deaths suggest that 504,000 people die each year because they engage in little or no exercise. Employing an identical formula, bad nutritional habits can be shown to account for 649,000 excess deaths annually. That is nearly 1.6 million deaths from only three causes—without considering alcoholism, accidents, poverty, etc.—out of 2.3 million deaths in 1995 from all causes combined. And on it goes—computer-generated phantom deaths, not real deaths—constrained neither by accepted statistical methods, by common sense, nor by the number of people who die each year.

Adjusting for Age at Death

Next and last, we turn to a different sort of deceit—one pertaining not to the number of smoking-related deaths but rather to the misperception that those deaths are somehow associated with kids and young adults. For purposes of this discussion, we will work with the far-fetched statistics published by CDC—an annual average from 1990 through 1994 of 427,743 deaths attributable to tobacco. Is the problem as serious as it sounds?

At first blush, it would seem that more than 400,000 annual deaths is an extremely serious problem. But suppose that all of the people died at age ninety-nine. Surely then, the seriousness of the problem would be tempered by the fact that the decedents would have died soon from some other cause in any event. That is not far from the truth: while tobacco does not kill people at an average age of ninety-nine, it does kill people at an average age of roughly seventy-two—far closer to ninety-nine than to childhood or even young adulthood. Indeed, according to a 1991 RAND study, smoking "reduces the life expectancy of a twenty-year-old by about 4.3" years—not a trivial concern to be sure, but not the horror that is sometimes portrayed. . . .

More Focused Studies Show Different Results

Perhaps that is why the Carter Center's "Closing the Gap" project at Emory University examined "years of potential life lost" (YPLL) for selected diseases, to identify those causes of death that were of greatest severity and consequence. The results were reported by R.W. Amler and D.L. Eddins, "Cross-Sectional Analysis: Precursors of Premature Death in the United States" in the 1987 *American Journal of Preventive Medicine*. First, the authors determined for each disease the annual number of deaths by age group. Second, they multiplied for each age group the number of deaths times the average number of years remaining before customary retirement at age sixty-five. Then they computed YPLL by summing the products for each disease across age groups.

Thus, if smoking were deemed to have killed, say, fifty thousand people from age sixty through sixty-four, a total of 150,000 years of life were lost in that age group—i.e., fifty thousand lives times an average of three years remaining to age sixty-five. YPLL for smoking would be the accumulation of lost years for all age groups up to sixty-five.

Threats Are Overblown

Amler and Eddins identified nine major precursors of preventable deaths. Measured by YPLL, tobacco was about halfway down the list—ranked four out of nine in terms of years lost—not "the number one killer in America" as alarmists have exclaimed. . . .

According to Amler and Eddins, even if we were to look at medical treatment—measured by days of hospital care—nonalcohol-related injuries impose a 58 percent greater burden than tobacco, and nutrition-related diseases are more burdensome as well.

Another statistic that more accurately reflects the real health repercussions of smoking is the age distribution of the 427,743 deaths that CDC mistakenly traces to tobacco. No doubt most readers will be surprised to learn that—aside from burn victims and pediatric diseases—*tobacco does not kill a single person below the age of 35.*

Nobody Dies Young Because of Tobacco

Each year from 1990 through 1994 . . . only 1,910 tobacco-related deaths—less than half of 1 percent of the total—were persons below age thirty-five. Of those, 319 were burn victims and the rest were infants whose parents smoked. But the relationship between parental smoking and pediatric diseases carries a risk ratio of less than 2, and thus is statistically insignificant. Unless better evidence is produced, those deaths should not be associated with smoking.

On the other hand, the National Center for Health Statistics reports that more than twenty-one thousand persons below age thirty-five died from motor vehicle accidents in 1992, more than eleven thousand died from suicide, and nearly seventeen thousand died from homicide. Over half of those deaths were connected with alcohol or drug abuse. That should put smoking-related deaths in a somewhat different light.

Most revealing of all, almost 255,000 of the smoking-related deaths—nearly 60 percent of the total—occurred at age seventy or above. More than 192,000 deaths—nearly 45 percent of the total,—occurred at age seventy-five or higher.

And roughly 72,000 deaths—almost 17 percent of the total—occurred at the age of 85 or above. Still, the public health community disingenuously refers to "premature" deaths from smoking, as if there is no upper age limit to the computation.

The vast overestimate of the dangers of smoking has had disastrous results for the health of young people. Risky behavior does not exist in a vacuum; people compare uncertainties and apportion their time, effort, and money according to the perceived severity of the risk. Each year, alcohol and drug abuse kills tens of thousands of people under the age of thirty-five. Yet according to a 1995 survey by the U.S. Department of Health and Human Services, high school seniors thought smoking a pack a day was more dangerous than daily consumption of four to five alcoholic beverages or using barbiturates. And the CDC reports that the number of pregnant women who drank frequently quadrupled between 1991 and 1995—notwithstanding that fetal alcohol syndrome is the largest cause of preventable mental retardation, occurring in one out of every one thousand births.

Can anyone doubt that the drumbeat of antismoking propaganda from the White House and the health establishment has deluded Americans into thinking that tobacco is the real danger to our children? In truth, alcohol and drug abuse poses an immensely greater risk and antismoking zealots bear a heavy burden for their duplicity.

Smoking Is Bad, But Not the Grim Reaper

The unvarnished fact is that children do not die of tobacco-related diseases, correctly determined. If they smoke heavily during their teens, they may die of lung cancer in their old age, fifty or sixty years later, assuming lung cancer is still a threat then.

Meanwhile, do not expect consistency or even common sense from public officials. Alcoholism contributes to crime, violence, spousal abuse, and child neglect. Children are dying by the thousands in accidents, suicides, and homicides. But states go to war against nicotine—which is not an intoxicant, has no causal connection with crime, and poses little danger to young adults or family members.

The campaign against cigarettes is not entirely dishonest. After all, a seasoning of truth makes the lie more digestible. Evidence does suggest that cigarettes substantially increase the risk of lung cancer, bronchitis, and emphysema. The relationship between smoking and other diseases is not nearly so clear, however; and the scare-mongering that has passed for science is appalling. Not only is tobacco far less pernicious than Americans are led to believe, but its destructive effect is amplified by all manner of statistical legerdemain—counting diseases that should not be counted, using the wrong sample as a standard of comparison, and failing to control for obvious confounding variables.

To be blunt, there is no credible evidence that 400,000 deaths per year—or any number remotely close to 400,000—are caused by tobacco. Nor has that estimate been adjusted for the positive effects of smoking—less obesity, colitis, depression, Alzheimer's disease, Parkinson's disease and, for some women, a lower incidence of breast cancer. The actual damage from smoking is neither known nor knowable with precision. Responsible statisticians agree that it is impossible to attribute causation to a single variable, like tobacco, when there are multiple causal factors that are correlated with one another. The damage from cigarettes is far less than it is made out to be.

Most important, the government should stop lying and stop pretending that smoking-related deaths are anything but a statistical artifact. The unifying bond of all science is that truth is its aim. When that goal yields to politics, tainting science in order to advance predetermined ends, we are all at risk. Sadly, that is exactly what has transpired as our public officials fabricate evidence to promote their crusade against big tobacco.

New Smokeless Tobacco Products Are the Same Old Killers

Stephen Jay

After years of protests and lawsuits against it, the tobacco industry is marketing new, seemingly safer, smokeless products to teenagers. Yet Stephen Jay's article claims that these new products are far from safe, and that Big Tobacco is once again singling out the most vulnerable members of society to make big money. Stephen Jay is professor of medicine, assistant dean for continuing medical education, and interim chairman of the Department of Public Health.

Taboka is just another in a long line of "new" tobacco products from Philip Morris since it was founded in 1881. Both Philip Morris and RJ Reynolds are feeling the erosion of market share in cigarettes and rushing to fill the void with products aimed at kids (their future) and that are a "substitute" for cigarettes in the increasingly smoke-free environments in the United States. RJ Reynolds has been test-marketing Camel Snus—another smokeless product—in Oregon and Texas. The choice of Camel was no accident, since Camel is a favorite with kids.

The marketing ploy of the industry has changed little in basic intent: to suggest to consumers that the product is "better and improved" with either explicit or implicit suggestions of improved safety—less threat to health. In the case of taboka, they are suggesting it as a substitute for smoking—when smoking is impossible (airplanes, smoke-free areas). The company is also suggesting (with no data whatsoever published in

Stephen Jay, "Tobacco Targets Youth: Tobacco Companies Looking for Lucrative New Markets Are Targeting Kids with Smokeless Products, Suggesting the Tobacco Products Are 'Safer'—Nothing Is Farther from the Truth," *Saturday Evening Post*, vol. 279, January–February 2007, pp. 70–71. © 2007 *Saturday Evening Post* Society. Reproduced by permission.

peer-reviewed literature) that taboka is either safer than other tobacco products or that it is "spitless"—a claim they currently make. Is it rational to believe that placing a bag equivalent to a small toxic waste dump between your gum and cheek would not produce "spit?"

Marketing Claims Do Not Adhere to Facts

In this largely unregulated industry, manufacturers can make any claims in their marketing promos without concern for the truth, facts, or science. We know that the "new improved and safer products" scare has worked brilliantly for the tobacco industry for 150 years. I wrote a brief letter in the journal *Tobacco Control*, an international peer-reviewed journal, which documented that tobacco companies in 1852 were removing the known toxic nicotine to market their products as safer—without the "poisonous" nicotine. I found this evidence serendipitously in an article in *Scientific American*. The ongoing debate among scientists and tobacco control experts today focuses on the trend of tobacco companies "fessing up" to the addictiveness and toxicity of tobacco and creating new products (both cigarettes and smokeless products) that may be safer—a practice referred to as "harm reduction." With smoking, you have major risks of lung and many other cancers. The cardiovascular risk ratios are also higher for cigarette smokers. With smokeless tobacco, you see oral cancers, major periodontal disease, and cardiovascular disease—increased blood pressure and risk of heart attacks.

In the United States, public health experts are skeptical of the science that purports to show smokeless is much safer than smoking—even if it is, experts worry about the law of unintended effects: Will the introduction of smokeless products increase or decrease smoking rates? With smoke-free ordinances and pressures not to smoke, will the widespread availability of new smokeless products provide a convenient way for smokers to continue their habit, thus decreasing smoking cessation? On the flip side, will young people today see the new products as a "safer" way to use tobacco? Since many smokeless users as youth migrate to cigarettes (the fastest way to get nicotine to your brain receptors), the question is, will these new products spawn new generations of smokers?

New Products Are Not Safer than Cigarettes

The bottom line is that without federal oversight of this industry, we will never really know the answers to these questions because the science will never be done to answer them. For example, the data that some scientists use as evidence of the relative safety of smokeless products is filled with methodological holes. One glaring hole is that no one knows what actually is in the smokeless or smoking products since the industry is unregulated. How can you do comparative research without knowing precisely what it is you are comparing? Second, none of the studies are prospective, randomized human trials.

My personal bias after looking at this evidence is that the overall premature mortality in lifelong smokers is greater than in lifelong smokeless users. But where I have a problem is in taking the above circumstantial evidence for less toxicity of smokeless and making national policy or endorsing smokeless as a safer alternative to smoking. This, I think, would be irresponsible. The U.S. Surgeon General has stated that smokeless is not a safe substitute for smoking. In Congressional testimony, former Surgeon General Vice Admiral Richard H. Carmona addressed the perception that smokeless tobacco is a good alternative to smoking.

"It is a myth. It is not true" Dr. Carmona stressed. "As the nation's Surgeon General my top responsibility is to ensure that Americans are getting the best science-based information to make decisions about their health. No matter what you may hear today or read in press reports later, I cannot conclude that the use of any tobacco product is a safer alternative to smoking. This message is especially important to communicate to young people, who may perceive smokeless tobacco as a safe form of tobacco use."

I agree with that statement.

The Antismoking Hysteria

Joe Jackson

An occasional smoker himself, Joe Jackson makes the argument that smoking bans and anti-tobacco propaganda are part of a new witch hunt. He acknowledges that smoking is detrimental to one's health, yet claims that the negative sides of smoking are vastly exaggerated, and that the antismoking campaigns have diminished everyone's democratic right to choose their own way of life. Joe Jackson is an English musician and singer/songwriter best known for the 1979 hit song, "Is She Really Going Out with Him?" and for his 1982 hit, "Steppin' Out." This article is an excerpt and the full version is available at www.joejackson.com.

Common Knowledge

It is has become 'common knowledge' that smoking is one of the worst things you can possibly do to yourself; 'all the experts agree'. Of course, 'all the experts' once agreed that masturbation caused blindness, that homosexuality was a disease, and that marijuana turned people into homicidal maniacs. In the 1970s and 80s British doctors told mothers to put their babies to sleep face-down. Cot deaths soared, until a campaign by one nurse succeeded in changing this policy, which we now know to have claimed something like 15,000 lives.

Most medical practitioners, institutions, and lobby groups are hard-working and well-intentioned. But they can just as easily be clueless, biased, or corrupt, not to mention increasingly, and worryingly, embedded with the pharmaceutical industry. Yet while presidents and prime ministers are routinely castigated as liars and crooks, it's rare to encounter even what I would describe as healthy scepticism towards health professionals. Why should this be so?

Joe Jackson, "Smoke, Lies and the Nanny State," www.joejackson.com, April 2007. Reproduced by permission.

I believe that we have to put our faith in someone, and that as our faith in political and religious leaders has declined, we have become not only excessively reverent towards doctors and scientists, but increasingly willing to allow them to dictate our lifestyles and laws. Health is seen as an unqualified good. Who can be against 'health'? Likewise, 'science' is equated with integrity and certainty. It has become our religion.

Unfortunately, there is precious little genuine science to be found in the pronouncements of media pundits and politicians. Instead we're fed a steady diet of 'junk science': facts out of context and out of proportion, insubstantial claims based on dubious methodology, and clever games with statistics. Like the perennial pub bore who holds forth with great authority on any number of topics, the average politician or newspaper editor tends to promote whatever 'science' suits his or her prejudice or agenda.

Things to Bear in Mind

I'm getting to the smoking issue, but I believe it's essential to start off by pleading for a much more sceptical attitude towards health authorities, not to mention people who use 'health' as window-dressing for their agendas. I'm also trying to disentangle emotional prejudice and fashion from reason. In the half-century I've been on this planet, I've seen no worse example of hopeless entanglement than in the debate—or lack of debate—over smoking.

Smoking has always been something which many people love and many others just don't *get*. As far as they're concerned, it quite literally stinks. They therefore tend to believe any horror story they hear about it.

There have also always been people who wanted to stop us smoking. A pretty dismal bunch they've been, too, from Sultan Murad IV of Turkey (who had smokers castrated) to Adolf Hitler [leader of Nazi Germany]. But whatever your personal feelings about tobacco, it's worth bearing in mind that antismokers have always exaggerated its dangers. They've always *had* to, since it's not enough to tell people—young people especially—that something they enjoy just might end up making them sick in, say, 40 years' time. But let's try to be more specific.

Lung Cancer and Convenient Numbers

We seem to be obsessed with cancer these days, perhaps because the idea that something is still beyond the power of doctors and scientists scares the living daylights out of us. I don't mean to trivialise; my father died of cancer. I do think, though, that we're overly zealous in our search for scapegoats (recent media reports have claimed that we can get cancer from hair dye, soft drinks and oral sex). I also want to point out—turning the negative into a positive for once—that cancer is mostly a disease of the old, and another reason it looms so large is that we're living longer and mostly healthier lives than at any time in history.

Lung cancer is the disease most strongly associated with smoking, though even this is a statistical rather than a causative link. In other words, it has been statistically shown that smokers are more likely to get lung cancer, rather than scientifically shown that the cancer is specifically caused by the smoking. This is a more important distinction than it might seem. Much of the antismokers' case is based on statistics, and statistics is not science.

It does make sense—so long as you don't mind bullying people out of their pleasures—to try to bring down the rate of lung cancer by getting people to quit smoking. But the evidence linking smoking with lung cancer is much less convincing than we are led to believe. For one thing, there is much disagreement about what the actual risk factor is.

The general consensus seems to reflect the pioneering studies of Professor Sir Richard Doll in the 1950s and 60s, which are still regarded as 'benchmarks'. Doll reckoned that about 160 in 100,000 smokers developed lung cancer as opposed to 7 in 100,000 nonsmokers; so you have about a 24 times greater risk if you smoke. This can also be expressed as '2,400%'. But beware of estimates of 'increased risk', especially when expressed in percentages; they're a good sign that someone is trying to frighten, rather than to inform.

If you buy 25 lottery tickets instead of one, your chances of winning go up by 2,500%. But though the number sounds impressive, your actual chances of winning are still minuscule.

Likewise, if Prof Doll was right, you still have a 99.8% chance of *not* getting lung cancer. This is nothing more or less than a re-presentation, or re-packaging, of the same data. But it immediately sounds a lot less scary. Especially if smoking is something you love.

More Inconvenient Numbers

Statistics always present one version of reality while leaving out many others. For instance: antismokers' increased-risk estimates leave out the fact that a majority of lung cancers happen within, or beyond, the normal range of death. In other words, if lung cancer is going to get you, it'll probably do so around the time when *something* is going to get you, whether you smoke or not.

There are also many contradictory statistics out there for those who care to look. Native Americans have half the rate of lung cancer of white Americans even though they smoke much more. Very few Chinese women smoke and yet they have one of the highest lung cancer rates in the world. Lung cancer rates practically everywhere have been rising since about 1930 and in some cases (e.g. American women) have not peaked yet, despite the fact that smoking rates have gone steadily down. Japan, one of the world's heaviest-smoking nations, is also in the top two or three in life expectancy. Japanese rates of lung cancer and heart disease have nevertheless been rising for the last 3 decades—at the same time as their smoking rate has gone down. Perhaps this is because their diet and lifestyle have become increasingly Americanised. I really don't know. All I'm saying is that 'inconvenient' facts should be investigated, rather than swept under the carpet.

The more you look into this sort of thing, the murkier it gets. Even the term 'smoker' is defined differently in different studies; some only look at heavy long-term cigarette smokers (there is very little risk in cigar or pipe smoking anyway) but others define anyone who has smoked 100 cigarettes in their life as a 'smoker,' others count as smokers people who quit 20 years before, and so on.

Antismokers maintain that smoking is responsible for about 90% of lung cancer deaths. But the Lung Cancer Alliance, a US lobby group, maintains that a half of lung cancer victims have never smoked.

All cancers have multiple risk factors (about 40 have been identified for lung cancer) and no one really knows why some people get sick and others don't. Lung cancer is the easiest disease to link with smoking, but even in this case, the danger cannot possibly be anywhere near as great as we're currently being told. Of course, many people have given up since the US Surgeon General's announcement, in 1964, that smoking could cause lung cancer. But no matter how many people quit, it's never enough for the antismoking zealots. This is why they've turned their attention more and more to:

The Smoking-Related Disease

This is one of the antismokers' cleverest invention. To say that a disease is 'smoking-related' is *not* the same as saying that it is directly caused by smoking, or that there is any actual proof of anything. It means simply that someone has decided that smoking *may be a factor* in that disease.

Over the last couple of decades, more and more diseases have been added to the list, often with very little evidence. Heart disease was one of the first, even though it has something like 300 risk factors, and some major studies (for instance, that of the citizens of Framingham, Massachusetts, which has been going on since 1948) have shown not only that the link with smoking is weak, but that moderate smokers have less heart disease than nonsmokers.

More recently it has become fashionable to blame smoking for just about everything, from 'clogging up' of the arteries (which happens to everyone as they get older) to blindness (well, they can't blame masturbation any more) to AIDS. It has also become fashionable, every time a smoker dies, to try to find a way to blame their death on smoking.

Recent media scares have claimed that smoking 'may' cause impotence or infertility. But people smoked more during the two world wars than at any other time in history, and what did we have in the 1950s? A baby boom! Other scares have found their way onto cigarette packets. 'Smoking causes ageing of the skin' says one. Well, maybe, for some people, but there are clearly more important factors, like the sun. And ageing.

The fact is that many statistics about smoking (and especially 'secondhand' smoke) are simply made up. For instance, until cervical cancer was recently proven to be caused by a virus, a completely random 13% of cases were attributed to smoking. Many of the estimates of smoking deaths are produced by one computer program. It's called SAMMEC (Smoking Attributable Morbidity, Mortality, and Economic Cost) and depending on which data you feed in, and which you leave out, it can produce pretty much any number you want.

The great thing about the 'smoking-related disease', is that it allows you to create the perception of a raging epidemic. The UK government says that 100,000 or 120,000 deaths per year (depending on who is speaking at the time) are caused by 'smoking-related disease'. The impression given is that these are all deaths specifically, and probably, caused by smoking, but it is no such thing. It includes nonsmokers who die of bronchitis or strokes, and smokers who die of heart attacks in their 80s. It includes people who quit smoking decades before. It is not exactly lying, but it is deliberately misleading, it is fearmongering, and in my opinion these people should be ashamed of themselves.

The Dose Makes the Poison

This is an old, but often ignored, scientific axiom. What it means is that there are safe and unsafe levels of *everything*. A little bit of arsenic is just fine. A significantly large amount of orange juice could kill you. But antismokers are now trying to sell us a scientific absurdity: that smoking is dangerous *at any level*.

It would seem obvious that there's a big difference between smoking five a day and fifty a day. Heaven forbid, though, that we should use our own common sense. In fact there is a great deal of evidence that moderate smoking—up to about ten a day—is not harmful, and indeed has clear benefits. Apart from pleasure (which current medical thinking deems irrelevant) it relieves stress, helps with weight control, and protects against or relieves the symptoms of quite a few diseases, including Alzheimer's, Parkinson's, ulcerative colitis, and cancers of the intestines and womb. Several doctors have admitted this to me in private, but you won't hear it from the medical institutions and lobby groups who have worked so hard to build smoking into Public Health Enemy No 1.

A couple of years ago I had the pleasure of meeting with the late Dr Ken Denson, head of the Thame Thrombosis and Haemostasis Research Centre in Oxfordshire, who was a rare and inspiring objector to what he called the antismoking 'witch hunt'. Dr Denson had devoted ten years to researching smoking, and published several medical journal articles eloquently arguing that the evidence, if looked at impartially and *in total*, was equivocal. He had unearthed countless studies showing that changes in diet could offset any risks, that moderate smokers who exercised had less disease than nonsmokers, and so on, and simply wanted to know why such studies were ignored while anything appearing to show the slightest risk was trumpeted from the rooftops. In Dr Denson's view, doctors were failing smokers by preaching zero-tolerance instead of balance and moderation. He also suggested that we talk about 'smokers-related', rather than 'smoking-related' diseases, since a majority of smokers have tended to have overall unhealthy lifestyles.

In Britain we're now being told that the working class and poor have much more disease than the middle class, and the main reason is smoking. But poorer and less-educated people are more likely to get poor health care, have bad diets, drink too much, work too hard, exercise too little, be more affected by stress and pollution, etc etc . . . all factors in 'smoking-related' disease which are impossible to separate from smoking itself. You can always single out something as the Curse of the Working Classes. In 1920s America it was booze; now it's tobacco.

P.A.S. (Pathetic Addict Syndrome)

Antismokers tell us that people only smoke because they are 'addicted to nicotine', and that most smokers actually want to quit. But most smokers enjoy smoking, and few people *want* to quit something they enjoy. Nag and frighten them enough, though, and you can certainly get them to believe that they *should*.

'Addiction' is not a clearly-defined scientific term, and it's very hard to separate 'addictions' from habits, rituals, or pleasures that we constantly repeat because they are, well, pleasurable. Probably everyone is 'addicted' to something: alcohol, sugar, caffeine, drugs both legal and illegal, sex, television, dieting, gambling, shopping, computer games, football, cars, or the gym. Of course, I recognise that some people find it hard to be moderate. But I think this is a question of personality, or perhaps genetic predisposition, rather than the 'fault' of the substance in question—or whoever sold it to you.

The Elizabethans who were the first European smokers observed that tobacco could become a habit which some found very hard to break. But, as Iain Gately points out in his excellent history of tobacco, *La Diva Nicotina*, they would have been baffled by our concept of 'addiction', since they believed that all human beings were granted by God the gift of free will. The idea that a man could be enslaved by a plant would have seemed to them absurd. I must confess this view makes more sense to me than the fashionable contemporary one which sees helpless victims everywhere, all needing to be protected either from themselves or from evil forces such as tobacco companies—who, conveniently, can then be sued for large sums of money.

Nicotine is not harmful. It is a naturally occurring substance present not only in tobacco but, for instance, tomatoes. The potentially harmful ingredients in a cigarette are tar and carbon monoxide created by combustion, along with various other common carcinogens and poisons at infinitesimal levels. (Note to you ex-hippies who've jumped on the anti-tobacco bandwagon: this is also true of other smokeables). Anyway, if nicotine is dangerous, why on earth are doctors trying so hard to sell it to us in the form of patches, gums and inhalers?...

Antismokers have to keep pushing 'addiction' since they either cannot believe, or cannot admit, that people not only freely choose to smoke but enjoy it. 'Addiction' also works to further stigmatise smokers by portraying us as contemptible junkies. Of course, if you're smoking out of pure compulsion and aren't even enjoying it, I would say you might as well quit. After all, if you're going to do something which not only has potential health risks but increasingly gets you treated like dirt, then you may as well at least get some pleasure from it. But many thousands have quit of their own accord, and many others are smoking moderately, or only at certain times, or switching to cigars. I meet these people all the time, but according to antismokers they don't exist. I personally only smoke when I'm having a drink. Perhaps I don't exist either.

How to Be Healthy

I think there are two different approaches to living a healthy life. One is to try very hard to avoid everything which current opinion holds to be bad for you, be guided by 'experts' and statistics, feel very guilty about any human imperfection, and generally believe that if you work hard enough, you can achieve invulnerability. This is very American. The other is to enjoy yourself, be reasonably moderate, be sceptical of the 'experts', and let the chips fall where they may. This approach is more European—or used to be. These are broad stereotypes, but they're both reasonable and most people are drawn more to one than the other. The problem comes when the first group starts to dictate to the second. Especially when there's no real proof, that either approach works best.

I believe the war against tobacco is part of a broader effort to turn us away from traditional pleasures, cures, and comforts, and to turn us into consumers of therapies and technical, or pharmaceutical, alternatives. We have, for instance, become overwhelmed by abstruse claims and counter-claims on the subject of nutrition. 30 years ago, we didn't even hear about 'nutrition'; instead we had something called food, which had worked pretty well for thousands of years. Now we all flail around in a minefield of polyunsaturated fats, antioxidants, amino acids, Omega-3, etc etc, so confused about the basic business of feeding ourselves that we are increasingly reliant on 'experts' to guide us. This is good business for the 'experts', but the rest of us have just ended up with not only more stress and anxiety, but more obesity and diabetes. . . .

What I'm suggesting here is that antismokers are, among other things, using tobacco as a scapegoat for health problems which have much more to do with diet and other factors. I accept that there is an element of risk in smoking. But 'Smoking Kills' is a meaningless statement, since you cannot prove that smoking is the specific and unique cause of *anyone's* death, and the vast majority of even heavy long-term smokers live to normal old age—as we can see from our own experience if only we stop allowing ourselves to be mesmerised by statistics.

I also don't think I should be coerced into quitting smoking, any more than I should be coerced into becoming a vegetarian or a teetotaller, even though I'd have a lower 'increased risk' of colon cancer in the first case and liver damage in the second. We are becoming a strangely risk-averse culture, and in strangely selective ways. Every prescription drug has potentially nasty side-effects, which kill thousands of people every year; but if we have a pain, or even just feel sad, we shrug our shoulders and take them. Thousands of people die every year in road accidents, yet we shrug our shoulders and get into our cars. When any risk is associated with a pleasure, though, we struggle to relinquish that pleasure, and we turn life into a stressed-out obstacle course.

This is perverse. Human beings are pleasure-seeking creatures. What is more conducive to health: pleasure or fear? Pleasure and free choice are not just 'nice work if you can get it'; they are crucial. Our doctors and politicians seem to have forgotten this, and are becoming mean-spirited and dictatorial as a result. . . .

Why I'm Bloody Furious

This is what it comes down to.

Firstly, I'm bloody furious that I, a responsible adult, am forbidden to have a smoke with a social drink—anywhere in the country. What makes me more furious, though, is that the [British] National Health Service is in disarray, with doctors and nurses being laid off, hospitals closing, and people waiting months for important surgeries; and yet they spend millions of pounds of taxpayers' money (my money!) on slick TV commercials, with Spielberg-esque special effects of sinister tendrils of 'secondhand smoke' enveloping innocent victims, to spread fear and intolerance and to depict smokers like me—with no good proof—as murderers.

I'm bloody furious that the USA fails to address major issues of terrorism, poverty, violent crime or environmental disaster, but spends well over a billion dollars a year on dishonest antismoking propaganda.

I'm bloody furious that AIDS, typhoid and dysentery are rampant in the developing world, and that more than 2 million children a year die simply from lack of access to clean water; yet the World Health Organisation spends millions trying to bully the comfortable citizens of prosperous countries out of their pleasures, when those citizens will live long and generally healthy lives anyway.

I'm bloody furious at the self-righteousness which accompanies the current antismoking climate when it is, is to a large extent, a political and economic phenomenon. The unprecedented success of the antismoking movement over the last 7–8 years corresponds directly to unprecedented infusions of cash from the Master Settlement Agreement and the WHO's pact with Big Pharma (in addition, of course, to punitive taxation and other less tangible forces such as 'political correctness'). Quite simply, the tobacco industry has been outmatched by a rich and powerful antismoking industry, whose tactics are about as righteous as those of the street fighter who, having knocked his enemy down, proceeds to give him a damn good kicking.

Every prohibitionist movement is essentially about power and profit, dressed up as health and morality. Any time a human pleasure can be shown to carry some risk, the doors are opened for those who want to tax, sue, regulate, legislate and discriminate. The story of Absinthe, for instance, parallels antismoking every step of the way: the same pseudo-science, selective and out-of-proportion propaganda, fearmongering, stigmatisation of the user, and largely unrecognised vested interests (in that case, the French wine industry).

Finally I'm bloody furious that 'public health' is rapidly accumulating powers which totally bypass the democratic process. This can be seen at many levels: Mayor Bloomberg's health inspectors have powers to enter and search which exceed those of the police (they have, among other things, raided people's private offices and fined them for the crime of Being In Possession Of An Ashtray). But it goes right to the top, with the WHO dictating policy to democratically-elected governments. Though it may strike some as a 'conspiracy theory', all the evidence suggests that health authorities and their pharmaceutical allies are establishing a supra-national nanny state which will increasingly dictate our lifestyles whether we like it or not....

Modest Hope for Change

I've painted a pretty bleak picture here, and I'm sure some readers will think: surely it's not that bad. Well, perhaps it isn't. I admit, for instance, that many antismokers are well-intentioned. But I have to call it as I see it: many are also ignorant, naïve, prejudiced, or just plain bullies. Some of the worst are the ex-smokers, who compensate for the loss of a love by turning it into a hate. Whatever their motivations, though, antismokers have used fearmongering and junk science to turn millions of people into scapegoats, and to build a powerful prohibitionist movement which has placed itself beyond criticism or accountability.

I take some comfort in the belief that while they're winning most of the battles, they can't ultimately win the war. You can't 'un-invent' tobacco, and there will always be many people who love it. A backlash will surely come: even now there are glimmers of hope. The Dutch parliament, unlike the

UK parliament, actually had a thorough and open-minded debate on ETS [Environmental Tobacco Smoke, also known as second-hand smoke], and in 2005 voted *against* a smoking ban. Instead the hospitality industry will manage the introduction of better ventilation and more nonsmoking areas by 2009. There was, however, *not one word* about this in the US or UK media.

In the near term, things will get even worse not just for smokers but for anyone whose lifestyles or habits are deemed to be 'risky' or 'unhealthy'. Those of us who want to resist need to get educated. There's no point in pleading for our 'rights'; as long as we're perceived as committing both suicide and murder, we don't have any. What needs to be addressed much more boldly is the antismokers' scientific dishonesty, as well as their conflicts of interest. These things are provable in a court of law.

In the meantime, party in whatever spaces they leave you, do whatever it takes to stay sane, and thanks for listening.

Big Tobacco Targets Youth, Minorities, and Women

American Heart Association

In this selection, the American Heart Association claims that the tobacco industry, in an attempt to open new markets, targets youth, minorities, and women. Hampered by lawsuits and a declining public image, Big Tobacco tries to market its products to new, and often vulnerable consumers. The American Heart Association is a national voluntary health agency whose mission is to reduce disability and death from cardiovascular diseases and stroke.

AHA Advocacy Position

The American Heart Association supports legislation that seeks to restrict or prohibit tobacco advertising, promotion and marketing to young people, minorities or women. The American Heart Association also works in partnership with the National Center for Tobacco-Free Kids on this important issue.

How Does the Tobacco Industry Target Youth?

The tobacco industry has long targeted young people with its cigarette advertising and promotional campaigns. One of the most memorable, the now-defunct "Joe Camel" campaign initiated by the R.J. Reynolds Tobacco Company, helped generate public outrage against tobacco company efforts to reach young audiences. In the November 1998 multistate tobacco settlement, the major tobacco companies promised not to "take any action, directly or indirectly, to target youth . . . in the advertising, promotion, or marketing of tobacco products." But

American Heart Association, "Tobacco Industry's Targeting of Youth, Minorities and Women." Reproduced by permission.

studies since then have shown that tobacco-industry marketing has reached record levels since the settlement, with much of the increase due to strategies aimed at young people.

In 1999, the first year after the multistate settlement agreement (MSA), the tobacco companies spent a record $8.4 billion on advertising and promotions, an increase of 22.3 percent from the previous year, the largest one-year increase since the U.S. Federal Trade Commission began tracking tobacco industry marketing expenditures in 1970. Then, in 2000, they increased expenditures another 14 percent to $9.6 billion. In 2001, the major tobacco companies increased their marketing expenditures to more than $11.4 billion, an increase in tobacco industry marketing of more than 66 percent since 1998. An August 2001 study in the *New England Journal of Medicine* showed that cigarette companies increased their advertising in youth-oriented magazines after the MSA was signed, especially for the three brands most popular with youth—Marlboro, Camel and Newport.

The National Survey on Drug Use and Health estimates that each day more than 4,000 people under 18 try their first cigarette. That's more than 730,000 new smokers every year. According to the Final Report of the National Commission on Drug-Free Schools, children and adolescents consume more than one billion packs of cigarettes a year. Economist Kenneth Warner, Ph.D., estimates that the tobacco industry needs to recruit 5,000 new young smokers every day to maintain the total number of smokers (due to the number of people who quit or die from tobacco-related illness each year). The Department of Health and Human Services [HHS] estimates that 90 percent of smokers begin tobacco use before age 20; 50 percent of smokers begin tobacco use by age 14; and 25 percent begin their smoking addiction by age 12 (the 6th grade). Since 1991, past-month smoking has increased by 35 percent among eighth graders and 43 percent among 10th graders, while smoking among high school seniors is at a 19-year high.

An April 1996 Journal of Marketing study concluded that children are three times more sensitive to advertising. According to a 1994 Centers for Disease Control report, 86 percent of underage smokers prefer Marlboro, Newport or Camel, the three most heavily advertised cigarette brands.

How Does the Tobacco Industry Target Minorities?

During the last decade, the tobacco industry has aggressively increased its advertising and promotional campaigns targeted at minorities. One of the industry's most notorious, and ultimately failed, minority cigarette marketing campaigns was for "Uptown" cigarettes. The American Heart Association, the American Cancer Society and the American Lung Association, working jointly as the Coalition on Smoking OR Health, played an active role in the Philadelphia "Coalition Against Uptown Cigarettes." The coalition brought health, consumer and social justice groups together to oppose the test marketing of Uptown in Philadelphia. R.J. Reynolds Tobacco Co., the manufacturers of Uptown, eventually withdrew the product under pressure from the coalition and HHS Secretary Louis Sullivan, MD. In addressing the issue of tobacco industry targeting of minorities, Dr. Sullivan said: "At a time when our people desperately need the message of health promotion, the tobacco industry's message is more disease, more suffering and more death for a group already bearing more than its share of smoking-related illnesses and mortality." Former District of Columbia Health Commissioner Reed Tuckson defined the tobacco industry's marketing practices as "the subjugation of people of color through disease." Recent studies have shown a higher concentration of tobacco advertising in magazines aimed at African Americans, such as *Jet* and *Ebony*, than in similar magazines aimed at broader audiences, such as *Time* and *People*. According to the Centers for Disease Control [and Prevention], in 1996 smoking rates among African-

American males had doubled within four years. From 1992 to 2000 smoking rates increased among African-American 8th graders from 5.3 percent to 9.6 percent; among African-American 10th graders from 6.6 percent to 11.1 percent, and among African-American 12th graders from 8.7 percent to 14.3 percent. Although African Americans tend to smoke fewer cigarettes per day and begin smoking later in life than whites, their smoking-related disease mortality is significantly higher.

Black-owned and black-oriented magazines receive proportionately more revenues from cigarette advertising than do other consumer magazines. In addition, stronger, mentholated brands are more commonly advertised in black-oriented than in white-oriented magazines. Billboards advertising tobacco products are placed in African-American communities four to five times more often than in white communities.

According to the National Coalition of Hispanic Health and Human Services Organizations, the tobacco industry specifically targets Hispanic consumers because of the long-recognized "economic value of targeting advertising to low-income Hispanics and non-Hispanic blacks," and because "Hispanics tend to be much more 'brand-loyal' than their non-Hispanic white counterparts." The Hispanic coalition also concluded "Billboards and posters targeting (the) cigarette message to Hispanics have spotted the landscape and store windows in Hispanic communities for many years, especially in low-income communities. Recent innovations have included sponsorship of community-based events such as festivals and annual fairs."

How Does the Tobacco Industry Target Women?

More than 178,000 women die every year from smoking-related diseases. Smoking among girls and young women increased dramatically during the 1990s. From 1991 to 1999, smoking among high school girls increased from 27 to 34.9

percent. Lung cancer has become the leading cause of cancer death among women, having increased by nearly 400 percent in the past 20 years. That statistic led former U.S. Surgeon General Antonia Novello to comment that "the Virginia Slims Woman is catching up to the Marlboro Man."

Ironically, since the 1980 Surgeon General's Report on women and smoking, the tobacco industry has stepped up the introduction of cigarette brands targeted to women. The new wave of marketing to women includes cigarettes advertised for their perfumed scents and exotic flavors or whose names include the terms "slims" and "lights." Product packaging and advertising have also featured watercolors and pastels.

One of the most egregious examples of the tobacco industry's targeting of women was the introduction of "Dakota" by R.J. Reynolds in 1990. An internal Reynolds marketing plan revealed that Dakota was to be marketed to "virile females" between the ages of 18 and 24 who have no education beyond high school and who watch soap operas and attend tractor pulls. At a 1990 Interagency Committee on Smoking and Health meeting chaired by the Surgeon General, the Dakota marketing plan was called a "deliberate focus on young women of low socioeconomic status who are at high risk of pregnancy." The target market for Dakota also happens to be the one group of women where smoking rates have declined the least and who are more likely than other women to continue to smoke during pregnancy. Cigarette companies continue to target women using themes in advertising that associate smoking with independence, stylishness, weight control, sophistication and power.

Why Do Teenagers Take Up Smoking?

Teenagers Imitate Characters on the Big Screen

Suzanne Batchelor

In her article Suzanne Batchelor examines the connection between tobacco use shown in the movies and teen smoking. She blames product placement and the favorable depiction of cigarette and cigar smoking from The Matrix *to* The Muppets *for many teenagers' decision to be "cool" and picking up a nasty habit. Suzanne Batchelor is a freelance writer on health-care issues.*

Watching popular movies is the No. 1 factor leading nonsmoking teens to light up, say researchers from New Hampshire's Dartmouth Medical School in a landmark 2003 study published in *The Lancet*. They found film character smoking more persuasive than traditional advertising, peer pressure or parents.

"Smoking in movies is having a major effect on health," concluded *The Lancet* editorial accompanying their findings. Given that the tobacco companies have agreed in settlements to cease marketing to the young, the question remains, how is it that the film industry has begun to release movies that give special play to lead figures who smoke?

No one seems to have any easy answers, but regardless of why movie characters are smoking, the health harm is the same.

Top Movies Show Tobacco Use

"There's a link between movie smoking and what kids do, and there's a lot of smoking in movies. It's extremely prevalent," said physician Michael Beach, who worked with Drs. Madeline

Suzanne Batchelor, "Movie Smoking Hooks Teens, Experts Say," *National Catholic Reporter*, vol. 40, February 6, 2004. Copyright © 2004 The National Catholic Reporter Publishing Company, 115 E. Armour Blvd., Kansas City, MO 64111. All rights reserved. Reproduced by permission of *National Catholic Reporter*, www.natcath.org.

Dalton, James Sargent and others on the Dartmouth study. Surprisingly, the researchers found the persuasive effect was strongest in children of nonsmoking parents.

Beach and colleagues also found that about 60 percent of the smoking in popular films was seen in the youth-rated movies (G, PG and PG-13).

Beach is typical of many tobacco control advocates and researchers who see:

- Attractive actors smoking identifiable brands on-screen, making tobacco control advocates fear for the health of a new, young generation of tobacco addicts;

- A tobacco industry that says it advertises only to adults who freely choose to smoke while the film industry keeps producing movies aimed at teens in which smoking is surprisingly widespread;

- Intriguing questions—but no answers—about how tobacco products get such big play in most top-rated and youth-rated movies.

To take the last point first: Among the top 10 box office movies reported for the week of Nov. 10—including "The Matrix Revolutions," "Elf," "School of Rock," "Mystic River," "Scary Movie 3," "Radio" and "Brother Bear"—only "Brother Bear" was smoking free. Characters smoke in more than two-thirds of youth-rated movies released in 2002 (movies rated G, PG and PG-13), according to a survey by Dr. Stanton Glantz, a professor of medicine, and analyst Karen Kacirk.

Most smokers begin as teenagers, researchers say, and smoking may be more addictive begun in those years when the brain is still forming.

"If you don't smoke by 18 or 21," Beach said, "the odds of starting as an adult are extremely small. It's getting these children through adolescence that's particularly important."

Only the Major Characters

The Dartmouth movie study didn't count the characters lighting up in the background, only cigarettes on the lips of major film characters. Researchers followed 2,600 children who had never smoked, ages 10 to 14, for one and two years, tracking which of fifty randomly selected top-selling movies they watched. Smoking by each film's central characters was measured.

Movie watching nearly tripled the risk a teen would start smoking, said Beach, who added, "What's surprising to some people is that movies can have that much impact." But is it? "Tom Cruise wore Ray-Ban sunglasses in one film and suddenly everyone has them." No surprise then at what results when "Julia Roberts and Sean Penn are seen smoking in movies."

Along with smoking, clearly visible tobacco brand names in movies are a major issue with anti-smoking advocates.

Health advocates point to the Marlboros smoked by Sam Rockwell in the 2003 film "Confessions of a Dangerous Mind," Sissy Spacek's Marlboros in "In the Bedroom," Russell Crowe's Winstons in "A Beautiful Mind," or John Travolta's Skoal in "Basic," to name but a few examples.

Product Placement Gets It Wrong

"Product placement" is an accepted form of advertising in which companies pay for movie exposure of their products. But paid product placement for tobacco products has been illegal since the signing of the 1998 Master Settlement Agreement. . . . No one has come forward with evidence of paid product placement of tobacco products since then.

Products might also appear as a matter of artistic expression or because they are integral to the plot of the story.

"In 'Men in Black II,'" said Beach, "you see the stars with a Marlboro carton. But when they open a refrigerator to get a jar of mayonnaise, the label on the mayonnaise is covered."

"If producers or directors use or depict our brands, they do so without seeking or obtaining our permission," said spokesperson Jennifer Golisch of Philip Morris USA, maker of Marlboros. "Our policy for over a decade has been to deny requests for use of our cigarette brands, name or packaging in motion pictures or television shows for the general public, irrespective of whether that audience is adults or minors."

The Church Weighs In

Catholic ethicists question Hollywood's attractive presentation of the harmful habit to adolescents.

"'Persuasion' we usually think of as the art of convincing somebody of something they're capable of thinking through, like persuading someone to vote for the candidate of our choice. This is different. We think it's something young people can't think their way through," says ethicist Carol Bayley of Catholic Healthcare West in San Francisco. "Then it's not free choice and it's not persuasion. It's something else."

Bayley said Catholic Healthcare West held tobacco stocks for many years, using ownership as leverage to urge tobacco companies to stop advertising to young people. "We ended up divesting of the stock because they just wouldn't change," she said. But, she added, widespread public opinion against such marketing might halt it.

Five years ago, one university professor began his own campaign, "Smoke Free Movies," and Web site. "Many women have told me they started smoking because of Olivia Newton John in 'Grease,'" said Stanton Glantz, professor of medicine at the University of California–San Francisco and a director of its Centre for Control Research and Education.

More than in the 1960s

When Glantz and analyst Karen Kacirk found there is more smoking in movies now than in the 1960s, his outrage led Glantz to create the "Smoke Free Movies" campaign, documenting the evidence frame by frame—Gwyneth Paltrow lighting Kools in "Great: Expectations" (1998), Johnny Depp smoking Lucky Strikes in "The Ninth Gate" (2000), stars such as Julia Roberts, Brad Pitt and Drew Barrymore exhaling smoke onscreen.

Glantz and Kacirk want Hollywood to rate "smoking" movies "R."

If an actor says the "F-word" twice in a film, or once in a sexual context (versus a single profanity exclamation), that film receives an R rating, explained Glantz. "I want tobacco treated as seriously as they treat the F-word."

Glantz criticized last year's Oscar-winner "Chicago" for its strong influence on teen girls. "In the 1920s about 5 percent of women smoked and the ones smoking were the rich ones, not the 'gun molls'—so the fact they were smoking at all was completely misleading. You have very high-profile actresses in a tremendously successful movie," said Glantz of "Chicago" stars Queen Latifah and Catherine Zeta-Jones, who smoke in the movie, as does star Richard Gere. "There's a lot of girls who are smoking now because of that movie and girls will start smoking for years because of that movie."

Glantz said the Smoke Free Movies group's ads and letter campaigns have provoked no explanation from the movie industry. "We do know smoking is there, that there's more than there used to be, yet everybody denies everything. That's nothing new," said Glantz. "Nobody is taking responsibility."

The U.S. Centers for Disease Control and Prevention in Atlanta found an increase in high school age smoking from 1990 through 1996, and that group continues to smoke, said Corinne Husten, a physician and chief of epidemiology at the center's Office on Smoking and Health.

"Each day, 6,000 children under 18 years of age smoke their first cigarette. Almost 2,000 of them will become regular smokers—that's 757,000 annually," states the American Lung Association Web site.

"If current tobacco use patterns persist, an estimated 6.4 million children will die prematurely from a smoking-related disease," the association estimates.

Seeing Smoking as Normal

Husten said movies subtly suggest, especially to the young, that smoking is normal. She mentions a 1999 study by the U.S. Department of Health and Human Services that found tobacco use in 79 percent of movies rated G or PG and 82 percent of those rated PG-13. That study, "Substance Use in Popular Movies and Music," was done by the Office of National Drug Control Policy and the Department of Health and Human Services' Substance Abuse and Mental Health Services Administration.

"To some extent, tobacco companies preach that it [smoking] is a choice, but if you're addicted to something, it's not really a choice," said Husten. "Most of the time people try to quit they're not successful. They find they're unable to quit. That points to a strong need to help adolescents understand it's dangerous to dabble."

"Young adults think they're in control, they can stop," said Sherry Marts, science director at the nonprofit Society for Women's Health Research in Washington. "A few might be able to but the majority of us, our brains are wired in a way that makes us susceptible to this addiction."

Smoking's persistence, Husten said, is aided by a key misunderstanding. "People probably get addicted much faster than we used to think," she said. "I think the power of addiction has been underestimated, and adolescents underestimate the likelihood that they themselves will become addicted."

Now Fr. Michael Crosby, a Capuchin priest, has joined Glantz's challenge to the movie industry. Head since 1980 of the tobacco program at Milwaukee's Interfaith Center on Corporate Responsibility, Crosby and allied religious orders have begun filing shareholder resolutions with major film industry leaders: Universal (and parent General Electric), Warner Bros (and parent Time Warner), Paramount (and parent Viacom) and Disney. Two-thirds of Disney's youth-rated movies show tobacco use, according to a survey of 2002 movies by Glantz and Kacirk.

Glantz calls the interfaith center's resolutions "a very big deal. The work Mike Crosby is doing is tremendously important."

Crosby's Midwest Capuchins and the interfaith center are joined by the Sisters of St. Francis U.S. Province (Milwaukee), Trinity Health (Detroit), Sisters of St. Dominic (Sinsinawa, Wis.) and Servants of Mary (Ladysmith, Wis.) in filing the shareholder resolutions against movie smoking.

"When you don't get anywhere communicating with management," Crosby said of past outreach to the film companies, "you have to go to the shareholders." Crosby said the interfaith center will publish ads to reach shareholders and generate public support in preparation for next spring's film industry shareholder meetings.

"How can anybody who is on the board of these companies who has teens or young kids themselves not understand this issue?" he asks.

Hanson, director of Santa Clara University's Markkula Center for Applied Ethics, said the ethical value of free choice may be trumped by tobacco's harm.

"It is particularly objectionable to target young individuals because of the addictive character of cigarettes," said Hanson. "If you can get them while they're vulnerable and not thinking as clearly, you can get them for life, except for a Herculean effort to extract themselves.

"A lot of Catholic thinking about issues like tobacco is based upon the concept of respect for the human being. Clearly, one is not respectful of the human body if one produces a product which used as intended produces harm to the body," said Hanson.

Tobacco Ads Seduce Teens

Kathiann M. Kowalski

In her article Kathiann Kowalski points out the many ways in which tobacco and cigarettes are sold as acceptable and even desirable to teens who are eager to copy fashion models and movie characters. From billboard ads to major movie productions, Kowalski finds that teens are under constant attack from those who have a financial interest in marketing smoking. Kowalski is an attorney and author who writes frequently for families and teens. Her articles have appeared in St. Anthony Messenger, Current Health 2, Straight, Odyssey, *and other magazines.*

"**N**o Boundaries. No Bull," reads the full-page cigarette ad in a recent issue of *Rolling Stone*. The tobacco company and its ad agency would say the rebellious tone of the in-your-face ad is not aimed at teens. But the magazine sits on the shelves of an Ohio public library's young adult/teen section. And the same issue carries a full-page ad for candy.

Coincidence? Probably not.

Crafty marketing? Almost certainly.

The Hook

For decades, tobacco companies have focused marketing efforts on teens. Why? Because companies want to replace older smokers who die from tobacco-related illnesses. As a 1981 Philip Morris document said, "Today's teenager is tomorrow's potential regular customer, and the overwhelming majority of smokers first begin to smoke while in their teens."

Relatively few people start smoking or switch brands after age 18. So tobacco companies developed ad campaigns to lure teens. Themes included rugged independence, freedom, popu-

Kathiann M. Kowalski, "How Tobacco Ads Target Teens," *Current Health 2*, vol. 28, April–May 2002. Copyright 2002 Weekly Reader Corp. Reproduced by permission.

larity, individuality, social acceptance, and carefree fun. Giveaways and promotional products became popular too. All these youth-appealing themes are still prominent in tobacco marketing.

In 1998, 46 states and the four major tobacco companies agreed to settle lawsuits for billions of dollars in tobacco-related health costs. The tobacco companies promised they would not "take any action, directly or indirectly, to target youth . . . in the advertising, promotion, or marketing of tobacco products."

The very next year, however, the money tobacco companies spent on magazine ads shot up 33 percent to $291.1 million. Sixty percent of that went for ads in youth-oriented magazines. Those magazines have at least 15 percent or 2 million readers ages 12 to 17. In 2000, magazine ad spending dropped back near presettlement levels to $216.9 million. Spending for youth-oriented magazine ads was still 59 percent. Tobacco ads in adult magazines such as *Time* reach many teens too. The Centers for Disease Control and Prevention (CDC) estimates that tobacco advertising reaches more than 80 percent teens.

"They're being heavily targeted by the industry," says Dr. Michael Siegel at Boston University's School of Public Health. "They need to resist and rebel against the tobacco industry's attempt to recruit them as essentially lifelong customers."

Dr. Siegel and his colleagues have documented tobacco marketing's success with teens. With cigarettes costing $3 or more per pack, price should play a big role in consumer choices. But the most popular brands among teens are the ones most heavily advertised.

Similarly, African-American teens tend to use the menthol brands advertised most in ethnically oriented magazines. "It's hard to explain the brand preferences of African-American youth on the basis of any factor other than advertising," notes Dr. Siegel.

Antismoking Ads May Have Failed

Even "anti-smoking" ads sponsored by the industry can give the opposite message. Some ads funded by tobacco companies stress how conscientious storeowners don't sell tobacco to underage buyers. An implicit message is that smoking is a "grown-up" thing. However, three-fourths of adults don't smoke. Likewise, ads about good works by "the people at" a large tobacco company ignore the disease, pain, and suffering caused by their products.

In Logan, Utah, a tobacco company gave away book covers that said, "Think. Don't Smoke." But, the word "don't" was a different color, notes 18-year-old Marin Poole, "So THINK SMOKE stood out." One design featured an angry snowboarder. "The snowboard looked like a lit match, and the clouds looked more like smoke than clouds," Marin says. Her campaign to get the book covers out of Logan High School, plus other anti-smoking efforts, earned her the Campaign for Tobacco-Free Kids' 2001 Youth Advocate of the Year award for the western region.

Cynthia Loesch won the award for the eastern region. In 1998, her group persuaded a major Boston newspaper to stop accepting tobacco ads. Cynthia continues to educate people—both adults and youth—about tobacco. "It's a fact that cigarettes do absolutely nothing for you, and all they lead to is illnesses and eventually death," says Cynthia.

Starstruck

Stars smoking in films or off-screen include Leonardo Di Caprio, Neve Campbell, Sylvester Stallone, Gillian Anderson, Ashley Judd, Sean Penn, John Travolta, and more. In a recent Dartmouth University study, young people were 16 times more likely to use tobacco if their favorite actor did. In another Dartmouth study, middle school students allowed to watch R-rated films (more inclined to show smoking and drinking) were five times more likely to try cigarettes and alcohol than those whose parents wouldn't let them watch R-rated films.

Even G, PG, and PG-13 movies often show tobacco use. In *The Muppet Movie*, for example, three cigar-smoking humans interacted with the Muppets.

"When movie stars are smoking in their movies or in front of young people, they're almost just as responsible as the tobacco industry is for addicting young people," maintains 17-year-old Shannon Brewer, the 2001 National Youth Advocate of the Year for the Campaign for Tobacco-Free Kids. "Whether or not they use it all the time, it's an influence on kids because it's saying that's what it takes in order to be that star."

Of course, not all actors smoke—and some take a stand against tobacco and other drugs. Actor Jeremy London, model Christy Turlington, and various other celebrities, for example, work with the CDC, American Lung Association, or Campaign for Tobacco-Free Kids to present positive role models.

Yet too many moviemakers use cigarettes and cigars as quick cliche props. "If they're creative producers and directors, they should be able to portray attractive characters through other means," challenges Dr. Siegel.

Why Should You Worry?

Very few legal products are deadly when used as directed. Tobacco, however, is America's No. 1 killer. According to the CDC, 430,000 Americans die each year from tobacco-related causes. Inhaled smoke and chewed tobacco directly affect the user. Secondhand smoke affects people who live, work, or socialize with smokers.

Nicotine is tobacco's addictive "hook." At least 63 of the other 4,000 chemicals in tobacco cause cancer, according to the American Lung Association. The list of toxic ingredients also includes tar, carbon monoxide, arsenic, hydrogen cyanide, acetylene, benzene, and formaldehyde.

Lung cancer and cancers of the stomach, pancreas, mouth, throat, and esophagus are all linked to tobacco. Tobacco also kills by causing heart attacks, strokes, and other circulatory diseases.

Besides direct deaths, tobacco makes people more susceptible to bronchitis, pneumonia, asthma, and other illnesses. Tobacco reduces lung capacity and impairs an athlete's performance. Smoking during pregnancy increases risks of miscarriage, premature birth, and sudden infant death syndrome (SIDS).

Tobacco messes with your mind too. Some teen smokers say smoking relaxes them. But researcher Andy Parrott at the University of East London found that teen smokers' stress levels increased as regular smoking patterns developed. Any perceived relaxation was just temporary relief of nicotine withdrawal between cigarettes. In short, cigarette smoking caused stress.

In another study reported by the American Academy of Pediatrics, teen smokers were nearly four times as likely as nonsmokers to develop serious symptoms of depression. Depression is a mental illness that hampers day-to-day functioning. Severe cases can even lead to suicide.

Beyond this, tobacco stains teeth and nails. It dulls skin and hair. Smoke reeks and lingers on hair and clothing. Instead of making people attractive, smoking does just the opposite.

Nasty Nicotine

About 60 percent of current teen smokers have tried to quit within the past year, reports the CDC. Most started out thinking they could quit at any time. But nicotine addiction seizes control before teens realize they're hooked—sometimes within days or weeks after the first cigarette.

Pure nicotine is deadly. Tobacco, however, delivers just enough nicotine (1 to 2 mg in the average cigarette) to hook users. You might say that cigarettes are engineered as highly effective drug delivery devices.

The National Institute on Drug Abuse reports that nicotine increases dopamine levels in the brain's "reward circuits" within 10 seconds of inhaling. The neurotransmitter dopamine increases feelings of pleasure. Nicotine also decreases the brain's levels of monoamine oxidase (MAO), an enzyme that breaks down excess dopamine.

Nicotine's peak effects dissipate within minutes. Users then need more nicotine to sustain the feeling. So, they smoke more. Depending on a person's arousal state, nicotine can be both a stimulant and a sedative.

When addicted users don't get nicotine, they experience withdrawal. Symptoms include cravings, anxiety, nervousness, and irritability. Thanks to nicotine, the tobacco industry often hooks customers for life.

Knowledge Is Power

Media messages that show tobacco favorably entice teens to smoke. But anti-smoking advertising can counter those influences. Dr. Siegel and his colleagues found that teens who regularly receive anti-smoking messages are twice as likely not to smoke as teens who don't get that exposure.

Instead of thinking that "everybody" smokes, teens were more likely to believe that only about one-fourth of American adults and teens smoke—which is true. In other words, getting the facts about smoking helps teens tell the difference between tobacco companies' media myths and reality, notes Dr. Siegel.

In fact, researchers at the University of Michigan found that from 1996 to 2001 the percentage of eighth graders who were smoking dropped to 12 percent from 21 percent; tenth graders who were smoking fell to 21 percent, down from 30 percent. Among 12th graders, the number of smokers dropped to 30 percent in 2001, down from a 37 percent peak in 1997. This drop in teen smoking is attributed to anti-smoking campaigns.

Anti-smoking ordinances and restaurant bans help too. Such rules reduce bystanders' exposure to secondhand smoke. Plus, they keep people from being constantly assaulted by tobacco's pervasive odor. "In towns that don't allow smoking in restaurants," notes Dr. Siegel, "kids are more likely to perceive that fewer people in their community smoke. They're not constantly smelling it and being exposed to it."

Take a Stand Against Tobacco

The more you know about tobacco and its consequences, the better prepared you'll be to resist media influences and peer pressure to smoke. Practice saying "No, thanks," or "I don't want to," in case a friend offers you tobacco. Better yet, say "I'd prefer if you didn't smoke around me. The smoke really bothers me." Real friends respect each other's wishes.

Whether you're 16 or 60, tobacco takes a toll on health. Encourage everyone around you to avoid tobacco. And be smart. Don't let the tobacco industry trap you.

Anti-Teen-Smoking Ads Make Cigarettes Desirable

Christopher Lee

To curb teen smoking, health officials and antismoking campaigns have spent millions of dollars to encourage teenagers to say no to cigarettes. Yet Christopher Lee argues that studies might have shown that ad campaigns have the opposite effect and dare young people to buy tobacco products. Christopher Lee is a Washington Post *staff writer.*

The surest way to get teenagers to do something is to tell them not to.

That principle appears to apply to some smoking-prevention ads created by tobacco companies, a new study has found.

Youngsters 12 to 17 were less likely to see smoking as harmful and had stronger intentions to smoke after the airing of television ads that urged parents to talk to their children about not lighting up, according to the study to be published in December [2006] in the *American Journal of Public Health*. The slogan of the national campaign, begun in 1999 by cigarette industry leader Philip Morris USA, was "Talk. They'll listen."

Researchers gauged the effect of the ads by analyzing television ratings from 75 U.S. media markets and data from an annual national survey of eighth-, 10th- and 12th-graders from 1999 to 2002.

Eighth-graders likely to have seen the ads targeted at parents were more likely to believe that the dangers of smoking had been exaggerated and more likely to say they planned to smoke, the study found. Older teenagers also expressed stronger approval of smoking and were more likely to have smoked in the 30 days before the school survey.

Ads Are Deficient

In the ads, "no reason beyond simply being a teenager is offered as to why youths should not smoke," wrote the researchers, led by Melanie Wakefield of the Cancer Council Victoria in Melbourne, Australia.

Smoking-prevention ads that tobacco companies targeted at kids themselves appeared to have no effect either way, the study found.

Dave Sutton, a Philip Morris USA spokesman, said the ads had been tested to make sure no unintended message was sent. Of parents who saw at least one ad, 61 percent talked to their children about not smoking, he said.

"We have found nothing through our research to indicate that the study's conclusions are valid," Sutton said. Still, the company is open to "collaborative dialogue" with public health experts on how to improve the campaign, he said.

Genetics and Mental Disorders Lead to Tobacco Use

Patrick Zickler

In this selection, Patrick Zickler reports that new studies have found that many teenagers might be predisposed to light cigarettes. While peer pressure and negative role models are often named as the number one explanation for teen smoking, genetics and mental disorders might influence young people's choice of whether or not to smoke. Patrick Zickler is a NIDA Notes staff writer.

By Patrick Zickler, *NIDA Notes* Staff Writer.

National Institute on Drug Abuse (NIDA)–supported scientists have found that a gene, called *DRD2*, partly determines whether an adolescent who takes a first puff on a cigarette will progress to regular smoking. Adolescents who carry one of the two known forms of the gene (*A1*) are more likely than those with the other variant (*A2*) to become daily smokers. If the teen also suffers from depression, the genetic effect is amplified, further increasing the likelihood of smoking escalation, according to Dr. Janet Audrain-McGovern and colleagues at the University of Pennsylvania Transdisciplinary Tobacco Use Research Center (TTURC).

The new findings result from a large-scale study that Dr. Audrain-McGovern and her research group undertook to clarify outstanding issues surrounding *DRD2* and smoking. Scientists have suspected for some time that variations in *DRD2* might influence people's responses to tobacco, based on the gene's function: It helps guide construction of sites where the neurotransmitter dopamine—which plays a key role in

Patrick Zickler, "Genetic Predisposition and Depression Both Influence Teen Smoking," *NIDA Notes*, vol. 20, no. 4, March 2006.

producing the pleasurable effects of nicotine—attaches to brain cells. Some previous studies have found that, indeed, men and women who smoked or were nicotine-dependent were more likely to have the *A1 DRD2* variant than the *A2*. However, other studies did not confirm the link.

DRD2 Variants and Smoking Progression

Dr. Audrain-McGovern's team recruited 615 adolescents (322 girls, 293 boys) to participate in their study. Because genetic diversity would increase the difficulty of interpreting results, all the youths were of European ancestry. Analysis of DNA obtained from cheek swabs showed that the frequencies of the alternative *DRD2* forms, or alleles, were roughly the same among the participants as have been seen in general population samples of people of European stock: Two-thirds (67 percent) had inherited the *A2* allele from both parents, 30 percent had one *A1* and one *A2* and 3 percent had two copies of the *A1*.

The researchers interviewed the teens in ninth grade, asking questions used in the Youth Risk Behavior Survey, including, "Have you ever tried or experimented with cigarette smoking, even a few puffs?" "Have you smoked at least one whole cigarette?" "How many cigarettes have you smoked in the last 30 days?" and "How many cigarettes have you smoked in your lifetime?" Based on their responses, the teens were categorized as never smokers, puffers (a few puffs, but never a whole cigarette), experimenters (at least one but fewer than 100 lifetime cigarettes), and current smokers (smoked in the past 30 days and 100 or more lifetime cigarettes).

The teens answered the same questions again in the fall and spring of their 10th-grade year and in the spring of their 11th-grade year. Analyzing the teens' sequential responses together with their genetic data, the researchers found no association between variation in *DRD2* alleles and the likelihood that participants who had never smoked would start, Dr.

Audrain-McGovern says. "However, among adolescents who had taken at least a single puff, we found a clear association between the *A1* allele and progressing up the ladder of smoking frequency—for example, moving from puffer to experimenter, or experimenter to current smoker. Each additional copy of the *A1* allele nearly doubled the odds of progression," she says. Among teens who had at least puffed once, those with a single *A1* allele were 1.8 times as likely, and teens who had inherited *A1* alleles from both parents were 3.4 times as likely as those with two *A2* alleles to progress to heavier smoking before they finished 11th grade.

"These results clearly illustrate the important interplay between a gene and the environment," Dr. Audrain-McGovern says. "The *DRD2* variant appears to play no role in whether or not these teens took that first puff. Its effect isn't seen until there is some biological exposure. Then, we see a markedly different response to nicotine, perhaps because the *A1* allele is associated with reduced density of dopamine receptors. If individuals with this allele have lower baseline levels of dopamine activity, they might experience greater reward when nicotine triggers an enhanced dopamine release."

DRD2 and Depression

During the ninth-grade interviews, the researchers administered the Center for Epidemiological Studies Depression Scale (CES-D Scale) to the study participants. Each teen rated how frequently he or she had experienced each of 20 depression symptoms during the past week. One hundred teens (16 percent) scored 23 or higher on this scale, which indicates clinically significant depression. Of the 100, 52 had at least one A1 allele. Teens without an A1 allele had an average CES-D score of 12.3; those with one *A1* and one *A2* had an average score of 15.1; and those with two copies of the *A1* allele averaged 16.7. There also was a significant association between the CES-D score and smoking status at the initial interview: The average score was 12.5 for never smokers, 14.6 for puffers, 13.7 for experimenters, and 20.8 for current smokers.

Teens with high depression scale scores and the *A1* allele were at the highest risk of smoking progression. Among teens with at least one *A1* allele, 33 percent of depressed teens, compared with 25 percent of nondepressed teens, reported smoking progression within 2 years.

The interaction of the *DRD2* allele and depression on smoking progression highlights the intricate interplay genetic, psychological, and social factors that influence adolescents' smoking behavior, observes Dr. Allison Chausmer of NIDA's Division of Basic Neuroscience and Behavioral Research. "This research group has previously shown that adolescents who have depression are more receptive than nondepressed teens to the messages contained in tobacco advertising. This is not a trivial number of potential smokers. Roughly one in five high school students has symptoms that represent clinically significant depression. Those who succumb to the appeal of tobacco manufacturers' advertising and have this particular genetic makeup may be more likely to progress to higher levels of smoking and ultimately experience consequences of reduced health and longevity."

How Do Teens Get Their Cigarettes?

Jessica Kuehne

If it is illegal for teenagers to buy cigarettes, then where do they get them? In this article, Jessica Kuehne examines this question, and concludes that the heavier the costs for cigarettes and the more difficult it is to obtain them, the more teenagers will lead smoke-free lives. Jessica Kuehne is a research assistant for the Campaign for TobaccoFree Kids.

More than half of all youth smokers usually buy the cigarettes they smoke, either directly from retailers or vending machines, from other kids, or by giving money to others to buy for them. Roughly a third typically get their cigarettes from others (usually other kids) for free, and a small but significant percentage of kids obtain their cigarettes by shoplifting or other stealing. But where and how youth smokers get their cigarettes can vary considerably from state to state or city to city depending on such factors as whether the jurisdiction strictly enforces the laws prohibiting tobacco sales to minors, requires retailers to keep cigarettes behind the counter, or has banned cigarette vending machines or restricted them to adult-only locations.

Nationwide, older youth smokers are more likely to buy their cigarettes directly than younger smokers, who are more likely to get their cigarettes from others or by stealing. Some of this difference is explained by older kids typically finding it easier to buy cigarettes than younger kids. But another powerful factor is that older youth smokers are more likely to be daily or regular users and regular or heavy smokers in all

Jessica Kuehne, "Fact Sheet: Where Do Youth Smokers Get Their Cigarettes?" *Campaign for Tobacco-Free Kids*, May 15, 2007. www.tobaccofreekids.org. Reproduced by permission.

youth age groups are much more likely to purchase their own cigarettes than kids who smoke less frequently or are only "experimenting." Not surprisingly, the older or more regular youth smokers who buy their own cigarettes are also major suppliers of kids who do not purchase their own cigarettes but get them from others.

Because of these purchasing and consumption patterns, the roughly half of all youth smokers who regularly buy their own cigarettes personally consume considerably more than half of all youth-smoked cigarettes. They also supply a substantial portion of the cigarettes smoked by those youth smokers who typically buy or borrow their cigarettes from others. As a result, it is likely that roughly three quarters or more of all cigarettes consumed by kids are purchased by kids—which is why strictly enforcing laws forbidding retailer sales to kids and raising cigarette prices through tax increases can quickly and significantly reduce youth smoking.

Research on How Kids Obtain Cigarettes

The 2006 *Monitoring the Future* survey found that 58 percent of 8th graders and 80 percent of 10th graders said cigarettes were easy for them to get.

The 2003 National Survey on Drug Use and Health (NSDUH) found that among 12 to 17 year olds who had smoked in the last month, more than three out of five (77%) had purchased their own cigarettes. More than half (53.3%) had directly purchased their own cigarettes, six out of ten (63.3%) had given money to others to buy cigarettes for them, three out of ten (30.5%) had purchased cigarettes from a friend, family member, or someone at school, and a small portion purchased cigarettes over the Internet or through the mail (2.6% and 2.9%, respectively). In addition, six out of ten (62%) had "bummed" cigarettes from others and more than one of ten (13.1%) had taken cigarettes from others without asking, with just under one percent (0.8%) had stolen cigarettes from a store. Older underage smokers were more likely to buy directly in stores than younger smokers. While there have been more recent NSDUH surveys, no questions on youth access have been asked since 2003.

The 2006 national Youth Risk Behavior Surveillance (YRBS) survey of 9th to 12th graders by the U.S. Centers for Disease Control and Prevention (CDC) found that 15.6 percent directly purchased their cigarettes from stores or gas stations, with a quarter of all 11th and 12th graders making such direct purchases. While the 2006 YRBS did not provide any additional detail, an earlier YRBS showed that 54.5 percent of those who had smoked in the past 30 days usually purchased their cigarettes directly from a store (23.5%), from vending machines (1.1%), or by giving money to others to make their purchases (29.9%). 30.4 percent usually borrowed their cigarettes from others and 4.4 percent usually stole their cigarettes. In addition, older kids and kids of any age who were daily smokers were much more likely to buy their cigarettes directly from stores than younger or infrequent smokers. No data was provided on the percentage buying their cigarettes from other kids.

The 2000 national Youth Tobacco Survey (YTS) found that among high school smokers, 32.2 percent usually obtained their cigarettes by purchasing them from a store and 25.1 percent usually gave someone else money to buy cigarettes for them—with 20.9 percent borrowing the cigarettes from others and 2.9 percent taking them from a store or family members. The 2000 YTS also found that 57.1 percent of high school smokers who have purchased cigarettes purchased their last pack of cigarettes by purchasing it from a gas station, 26.3 percent from a convenience store, and 7.7 percent from a grocery store. No data was provided on the percentage buying their cigarettes from other kids. No additional YTS data on the specific sources of cigarettes for youth has been released since the 2000 YTS. But the 2004 YTS showed that 70.6 percent of middle school smokers said that they were not asked to show proof of age when trying to buy cigarettes from a store. 66.4 percent said they were not refused purchase of cigarettes due to their age.

A 2006 study conducted in the Memphis [Tennessee] city school system found that even among 11 and 12 year-old seventh-graders, 11 percent were able to purchase their cigarettes from stores. In addition, 30 percent got their cigarettes from friends, six percent from vending machines, and 17 percent stole them.

Making It More Costly or Difficult for Kids to Buy Cigarettes Reduces Youth Smoking

Numerous research studies have found that making obtaining cigarettes as inconvenient, difficult, and expensive as possible for kids not only reduces the number of kids who try or regularly smoke cigarettes, but also reduces the number of cigarettes consumed by kids who continue to smoke. Because youth purchases are the major source of cigarettes smoked by kids, increasing cigarette prices and minimizing the number of retailers willing to illegally sell cigarettes to kids have each been shown to reduce youth smoking. While these measures directly affect youths who buy their own cigarettes, they also reduce the number of kids who buy cigarettes and supply them to other kids for free. Price hikes may also make it less likely that parents and other adults will give cigarettes to kids, be as careless about leaving their cigarettes where children can easily take them, or not notice when some of their cigarettes are missing.

In contrast to retail-enforcement efforts, voluntary tobacco industry programs to reduce illegal retailer sales to kids have not been found to reduce youth sales effectively. Similarly, while total bans of vending machine cigarette sales will eliminate that source, kids still readily obtain cigarettes from vending machines in those jurisdictions that restrict vending machine sales to adult-only locations or otherwise regulate vending machine sales without eliminating them.

Hip-Hop Images Cause Minority Youth to Start Smoking

Associated Press

This selection argues that the cool images of hip-hop artists smoking seduces minority teenagers into buying cigarettes. Smoking has always been closely linked with certain cultural attitudes or movements, and infusing tobacco ads with pictures of music artists makes smoking acceptable and even desirable to the targeted audiences. The Associated Press *is the largest and oldest news organization in the world, providing news, photos, graphics, audio, and video to media outlets around the world.*

The colorful images on the boxes of Kool cigarettes depict the urban nightlife. On one, a disc jockey scratches a record. On another, people are captured dancing mid-bounce.

Other trendy cigarette brands feature a blend of menthol tobacco with flavors like berry, mocha, coconut or lime.

The latest cigarette marketing efforts have caught the attention of health officials and anti-tobacco activists, who are accusing tobacco companies of using hip-hop images and attractive flavors to seduce minority youth into smoking.

"What adult that you know prefers a tropical or berry-flavored cigarette?" asked Sherri Watson Hyde, executive director of the National African American Tobacco Prevention Network. "One wonders if we're talking about a cigarette or Lifesavers or Now & Later."

Health officials gathered in August in Atlanta to voice "our opposition to the attempts of the tobacco industry to seduce our youth using the appeal of hip-hop culture," says Dr. James Gavin III, president of Morehouse School of Medicine.

New Products Are Catered to 'Cool' Youths

Representatives of the American Legacy Foundation, the National African American Tobacco Prevention Network, the National Latino Council on Alcohol and Tobacco Prevention, and Morehouse called for cigarette makers to remove the products from stores, especially in minority communities.

The new Kool Mixx, Kool Smooth Fusion and Camel Exotic Blends—all from the R.J. Reynolds Tobacco Co.—and Philip Morris' Marlboro Menthol 72mm are being heavily marketed to youth in Black, Hispanic and other minority communities, the activists said.

They accused tobacco companies of using flavored cigarettes to draw children who are not used to the taste of a regular cigarette.

"It's hard to believe that these sweet-tasting products are not targeted to youth," Iowa attorney general Tom Miller said in a prepared statement. "That the tobacco companies can say otherwise with a straight face is down-right appalling."

Kool ads have appeared in Black magazines such as *Ebony*, *Essence* and *Vibe*, which included in its April issue a CD-ROM that blended the Kool Mixx brand with hip-hop music.

Kool's marketing campaign is being fought in several states. Maryland, New York and Illinois have lawsuits pending against Brown & Williamson, which merged last month with R.J. Reynolds Tobacco Co., for its Kool Mixx ad campaign. Chicago-area activists protested a Kool-sponsored DJ competition in May.

Tobacco companies said in August they would not pull the cigarettes from store shelves because they have done nothing wrong. They say they remain in compliance with their 1998 settlement with state attorneys general, which prohibits the marketing of tobacco products to youth.

Targeting Teenagers Is Key to Tobacco's Success

The Kool ads are aimed at people ages 21 to 34, not children, and the average Kool brand smoker is White and 45 years old, says Reynolds spokesman Mark Smith. The brands are offered in stores across the country, not just certain communities or neighborhoods.

"The urban experience is what these brands are aiming toward—the consumers of the products reflect that," Smith said. "We've been doing the hip-hop stuff for six years. Most consumer goods companies are doing the same thing."

The problem is that children, especially teenagers, aspire to appear three to four years older than they actually are and pay attention to older people's dress, lifestyle and behaviors, says Terry Pechanek, associate director of science for the Centers for Disease Control and Prevention's Office on Smoking and Health.

Health officials have been working to reduce the number of child smokers because four out of every five smokers say they started before age 18. Smoking, the top cause of preventable death in the country, kills about 440,000 people a year, including 45,000 Blacks, through heart disease, stroke and cancers.

"If our youth never started smoking, these numbers would dramatically decline," says Dr. David Satcher, a former U.S. Surgeon General and the director of the National Center for Primary Care at Morehouse School of Medicine.

CHAPTER 3

Perspectives on Smoking

Quitting Smoking Makes Me Sick

Susan Shapiro

*In this memoir Susan Shapiro chronicles the perils of quitting to-
bacco. With wit and humor she describes what it feels like to
give up an addiction, while trying to live a healthier life. Shapiro
has written for many newspapers and magazines. She is the author of the memoir* Five Men Who Broke My Heart.

1 0 A.M.: Woke up and stuck nicotine patch on my arm, determined to once and for all quit cigarettes. Wrote list of
reasons: live seven years longer, please my husband Aaron,
have healthy children, be socially acceptable. Tore up list and
made better one: look younger, have fewer wrinkles, spite en-
emies. Scratched patch, which itched like hell. Went out to
buy carrots, celery, grapes, ten packs of Juicy Fruit, lollipops,
and rice cakes. Finished it all by 11 A.M., desperately craving
cigarette. Went back out though it was pouring rain. Bought
four packages of fat-free Entenmann's brownies. Tried to work.
Instead polished off brownies and took nap.

12:30 P.M.: Woke up feeling ill from brownies and cold
caught walking in rainstorm. Took a Sudafed. Felt better. Felt
delirious. Tried to work, but couldn't concentrate on anything
but wanting to smoke. Read in newspaper that schizophrenics
and manic-depressives in mental hospitals committed suicide
when their cigarettes were taken away. Decided never to have
children. Called brother Brian, the trauma surgeon, who'd
been sending X-rays of cancerous lungs, asking him to send
65 more nicotine patches. Took another Sudafed. Was there a
Sudafed group in the city?

2 P.M.: Tried to work. Developed bad cough and sore throat. Read another newspaper, scanning obits for people who died of lung cancer, happy to see one in his sixties. Took another nap. Dreamed I was stuck in the middle of a tidal wave and lit up, then felt sad I fell off the wagon. Woke up and found I wasn't smoking but wanted to be. Remembered that my friend Irene warned me about weird patch dreams. Called my cousin Miranda, who said that after she quit, her concentration didn't come back for a year. Took one hundred deep breaths. Breathing was overrated. Read touching article on recovery mission at Ground Zero, noting only that rescue worker in picture was smoking. Felt exhausted though I had just slept, read, and eaten all day. When it stopped raining, took a walk, counting that nine stores and bodegas on the block sold cigarettes. Called my friend Roger, who said, "My neighbor quit in three days on Nicorettes. Try Nicorettes," though I told him I tried them and threw up, then went out and smoked two packs to get the taste out of my mouth. Read that nicotine's harder to quit than heroin. Took another Sudafed. Thought about smoking. Brian called back to say don't even think about smoking with patch on, somebody's fingers fell off.

4 P.M.: Spent twenty minutes on exercise bike. On *Oprah*: "Mothers Who Want Their Violent Kids Taken Away" put problem into perspective. Called my sister-in-law Monica, who complained every time I took out a cigarette for twenty years but now said, "I can't talk to you when you're like this, you're too intense." Tried to work but realized it was impossible to be a freelance writer, nonsmoker, and thin in the same year. Sudafed was losing its bite, e-mailed Aaron to pick up Comtrex on his way home from work. Negotiated self-destructive behaviors: decided that taking sleeping pill, smoking a joint, getting drunk, and making myself come was better than a cigarette and Oreos, though not if done on the same night.

5:30 P.M.: Felt depressed and edgy, sweating and coughing up phlegm. Hand shook while reading another paper, where tobacco company executives said nicotine wasn't addictive. Made list of ten seventy-year-old smokers still alive. Had dinner with Irene, who kicked habit and gained twenty-four pounds in four months, sure it was the smart choice. Considered heroin. Stopped at Duane Reade to buy pacifier, pretending it was for my two-year-old niece. Pondered how anyone could expect morality from people who plastered penis-faced camels all over the country. Bumped into novelist pal Kathy, who blew smoke in my face while saying, "it's great that you're stopping." Tried to come up with one famous writer who didn't smoke or drink.

6:30 P.M.: Forced myself to gym. Did high impact aerobics, weight machines, sat in steam room, had a Swedish massage. Walked out of health club, longing for cigarette. Glared at smokers on street, enraged they looked so beautiful and happy. Added up money saved from not smoking. Spent $100 on Swedish massage, $46 on way home for seven boxes of fat-free cookies, twenty-seven cinnamon sticks, and three Lean Cuisines. Snapped rubber band around wrist one hundred times. My father the oncologist e-mailed, "The patch doesn't really work," forgetting that the last time he quit his thirty-five-year three-pack-a-day habit he gained thirty-five pounds and smoked a six-inch cigar every night. Decided neurosis was genetic. On stationary bike watched *Saturday Night Live* rerun, which quoted tobacco company execs saying that the 400,000 annual smoking-related corpses weren't really dead. Downstairs neighbor complained bike made too much noise. Did serenity exercises. Pictured sitting on a tropical beach, where I was happily smoking.

8 P.M.: Ate more celery, fruit, salad. Polished off Oreos. Felt bloated and constipated, dying for cigarette. Aaron came home with Comtrex and roses to congratulate me on my first smoke-free day. Burst into tears. "Maybe you want to call Dr.

Winters?" he asked. Screamed, "No! F--- you!" Unable to sleep all night, wondering why I was perfectly healthy smoking two packs a day for two and a half decades but got so sick on the day I quit.

Don't Turn Smokers Into Criminals

Shawn

In this text, Shawn, who hates smoking but enjoys an occasional cigarette, argues that people in a democratic society should have the right to decide whether or not to smoke in bars and restaurants. He denounces smoking bans as undemocratic and defends the right of everyone to choose whether or not to smoke. Shawn argues that smoking is only one of the many choices we make with respect to our health and well-being, and that the law does not have the right to take away that choice.

I am a 19 year old teenager in college and I don't smoke. Actually, that is what I tell my doctors and friends and that is what I say when people ask me that. But, the truth is that I smoke on occasion, but I think that really amounts to a, "No, I don't smoke."

I have always been a walking hypocrite in many ways. I absolutely hate people who smoke, I refuse to date people who smoke, and I make sure I surround myself with people who don't smoke. Cigarette smoke in restaurants detests me and I think there should be a law in every state, not just some, that says you are not allowed to smoke inside restaurants. However, I do on occasion, probably once a month or so, take out my pack of Marlboro Lights and light up. I know very well the side effects that could come from it and I was taught at a very young age to "just say no." I always just smoke one and I have never ever had the craving to have another.

Let People Decide for Themselves

However, I do believe that people should have the right to choose whether or not they want to smoke. We all know the arguments. Smoking is cool and it will make you look older, but it will give you lung cancer, put a hole in your throat, and probably be the cause of your death. We all watch TV and see the truth.com commercials urging us not to smoke and we all see the movies where some hot actor or actress is lighting up. The reason why I think we should all have the right to choose whether or not we want to smoke is because not only is it our right to pick, but also because we are given all the information we need at our feet. We very well know the good and bad about smoking. It calms you and makes you not hungry anymore, but kills. Given this information, I think we should be able to pick for ourselves whether or not we want to smoke.

I disagree completely about finding your child's cigarettes to just throw them away. I know for a fact that if my parents just threw away my cigarettes that would make me want to smoke cigarettes even more just to anger them. What parents need to do if they find their child smoking is to actually talk to them and help them get a more active life. With a more active life, their child will be too busy to smoke and will spend less and less time thinking about it.

Smoking in Cars Should Not Be Banned

There has been a lot of talk lately about drivers smoking in their cars with the windows down. I have been driving for over three years and I know that I absolutely hate when I am at a red light waiting for it to change and there is a smoker in the car right next to me. On the radio the DJ did a show about whether people think there should be a ban on it or not. Most people said yes because they don't want the children in their car to have to deal with the second hand smoke. However, as much as I hate second hand smoke, I think drivers have their own free choice of smoking in the car. Think about it this way, if they don't smoke in their cars, it would make them smoke in restaurants and personally I would much rather not have to deal with that in restaurants. If a driver who smokes pulls up next to you, simply put up your window. It is not that difficult and nowadays with power windows, you don't even have to move more than a couple inches. Our cars come with windows for a reason and the recycle air button to filter that smell out of your car.

Freedom Is More Important than a Smoking Ban

Americans all fight for the freedom of choice of voting and abortions. Smoking is just another choice we make. The choice to smoke is in many ways similar to the choice of voting. Some of us vote while others choose not to just like some choose to smoke and others don't. However, for every person that votes Republican or for every person that votes Democratic, the opposite party gets hurt just like second hand smokers get hurt. But, with second hand smoke, you have a choice. If there is a smoker near you, just get up and leave. It is not a big deal, nor is it a lot of effort on your part. I say, let the smokers smoke all they want. In the end, it's only natural selection at work.

I Love Smoking—But Not Enough to Do It

Anna Pickard

Anna Pickard, who keeps a blog, writes about her love for smoking, and about the many small details she loves about it. And yet, one day, almost by accident, she stops, and the next day she refrains from smoking again. Day by day, she expects to light another cigarette, but in the end does not. She comes to see her behavior as being dictated by her addiction and slowly works her way to a smoke-free life. She does hate smoking, but she doesn't need the habit anymore either.

The fact is, I like smoking.

Oh, I like smoking for lots of reasons. Lots.

- I like smoking because of the rush of adrenaline you get when you get a good pull on your roll-up. The smoke coursing into your lungs, the immediate relief as the nicotine feeds into your bloodstream. I like the physical sensation of it.

- I like smoking because I'm shy, and rolling cigarettes calms me down and allows me to focus my attention somewhere else, making me feel less self-concious. I like the fact that if I'm *extremely* unsure of myself and stuck in a situation where smalltalk or self-confidence is called for, I can always excuse myself and run outside and smoke, quietly.

- I like smoking because it's always been a good way of meeting people. I like the fact that people tend to start talking to each other when they're huddled out in the

Anna Pickard, "I Like Smoking," *Little Red Boat*, February 5, 2006. © Anna Pickard. Reproduced by permission.

cold doing something nefarious and anti-social. And yes, I tend to like the kind of people who smoke. I don't know why that is, I just do.

- There just isn't anything much nicer than a coffee and a cigarette after a meal. There just isn't. Sorry.

Yes, I like smoking.

I like smoking, and I like cigarettes.

So it's a bit of a shame for me that I haven't had a single one in over three weeks then, I suppose.

Stringing Together Smoke-Free Days

A few weeks ago, there was a night out in the pub with a friend, during which I had smoked my usual 400,000 roll-ups. Then next day, I didn't go out at all. This is not unusual. I am a hibernating thing, and am generally happy to not go out as long as there is food and internet and telly and books to hand. And bed. Anyway. I didn't go out of the house, and as I have never smoked in the house, I didn't smoke. Day one.

My beloved had just arrived back from one of his business trips, and we'd both taken the Monday off, as it was the first time we'd seen each other for a bunch of time. We didn't leave the house—so I didn't smoke. Day two.

I woke up on the morning of day three and decided that I wasn't smoking any more.

I put the tobacco in my bag as usual. I had my lighter in my pocket. On the bus, I rolled my 'walk-to-work' cigarette as usual. I got off the bus, put it in my mouth, and flicked my lighter. Again. And again. It wasn't working. I was passing a bin, and a newsagent. I prised the cute little rollie from between my as-yet unconvinced lips, and threw it in the bin. The lighter followed it.

I had another one in my pocket, I realised, three steps later. But I didn't roll a cigarette to be lit by it. No I didn't. The moment had passed.

All day I sat at my desk. Knowing that in my bag was the last of my duty free from Sri Lanka—a full, huge packet of tobacco that would make me several weeks-worth of rollies. When everyone left the office at the end of the day, I stood over the bin and tipped my tobacco into it.

I apologise to anyone sitting there screaming 'You bitch! I could have had that!'—but I needed to do it. If I'd given it to someone, I always would have felt like I could have asked for some back later on—and they might always have felt like they should give me it if I asked. I went home, in a foul mood. I hadn't smoked at all. Day three.

For three more days I walked around in being a complete cow. Everyone, without exception, was an idiot and a general waste of *a)* skin, and *b)* my time. So I told them so.

I felt a bit bad, but not very. My beloved begged me to smoke. I told him he was an idiot.

This was the problem. Because I liked smoking. And I liked cigarettes. And I liked smokers, I just didn't like the person I became when I hadn't had a cigarette in a while. I didn't like the fact that I was addicted, and everyone else had to pay.

I Wanted to Become a Different Person

As I said, quite often I would go for a day without one. And by the end of it I would be grumping at my beloved, or crying, or storming about, and he would never be able to work out why, because he has never smoked, and even though I might tell him why it happened one week, he would forget by the next. Because he has to remember lots of important things, so the other things get pushed out. And also he has, in general, the memory of an intelligent garden ornament. This is lucky, as it is still better than mine, so we are perfect for each other.

I didn't smoke all that week though. Nor the next. Stupid things started happening. Things that make me sound like a non-smoking evangelist—and I promised I'd never be one, and I won't, I swear, but it's been incredible and I have to write this down somewhere.

I started running for the bus. Just little spurts of running. Things that I wouldn't do two weeks previously because I got so embarrassed of how out of breath it made me.

I started getting off the bus early and walking the rest of the way in. When I got there, I would walk up the five floors to my department when I arrived in the morning. At the end of the day, I would walk some of the way home again.

This wasn't a conscious decision. This wasn't part of a healthkick. It was just because I had so much energy I couldn't see how else to get rid of it. And yes, I was amazed. I was breathing.

Facing Temptation

On a Saturday night, we went to a birthday party in a pub. I knew I was going to cave in and smoke. I knew that I was going to be sitting with friends who would be compulsively rolling all night, just as I would have done. I knew that at some point, some time between the third and fifth pint, I was going to smile sweetly at someone, then lean over and take a pinch of their tobacco and one of their papers, nick a small piece of Rizla packet for the roach, and roll myself a little tube of lovely.

And then I didn't. Believe me, no one was more surprised than me. Except possibly my beloved. And my sister. But I was pretty surprised. I bounced home.

I don't understand. I've lost my confidence prop, but I've actually seemed to do something good to my confidence. I've decided something and actually kept to it. This is unusual. It feels good.

It feels good. My decision. My decision to 'just not be smoking at the moment'.

Yes, I know, it's a bit of a crap decision. But let's face it—I might smoke again some time in the future. Some time when

I'm not addicted anymore and can just have a random ciga-rette, at times of pressure or when having that cup of coffee after that meal. When I can smile sweetly and take a pinch of tobacco from someone else's pack—as other ex-smokers have so often smiled sweetly and taken from mine.

So I've decided just not to smoke at the moment. It's a good decision, I think.

And to be honest, I don't want to decide to give up.

Because really, at the end of the day, I like smoking. I just don't do it much anymore.

I Might Die Early, but at Least I'm Cool

George Meluch

In this essay George Meluch takes aim at the many antismoking campaigns. The hysteria, he claims, produces in him not the wish to quit, but to light his next cigarette. While he acknowledges that smoking is bad for one's health, he is also adamant about his right to smoke. Smoking might rob him of years in good health, but he doesn't want to be lectured about the choices he makes for himself. Meluch is an artist and essayist.

Nothing fills me with the need for a long, smooth drag of a cigarette like watching several thousand teenagers play dead in front of a corporate tobacco office. What the kazark is wrong with this "Millennial generation?" They wear clean, brightly colored yet conservative clothing, they have a deep sense of National identity and they hate smoking and drugs.

Most irritating of all is the Truth campaign, with its fluorescent construction-zone orange theme color and sickeningly righteous handprint logo. The Truth campaign has joined the evils of advertising with the annoying group-mindedness of teenagers to bring us the most insipid anti-smoking guilt drive yet. The ad campaign has bored us with sentimental and macabre live performances using masses of teenagers and has confused us with public art pieces. Most recently thirty ice statues of pregnant women with baby-dolls inside their hollow stomachs were left to melt in the New York sun.

The ads all have the same effect on me. "Must . . . have . . . *cigarette!*"

Smoking Is a Form of Suicide

It's not my rebellious generation X attitude towards life and public service messages that has me locked in my life-sucking addiction, but it bothers the hell out of me that teenagers believe it's necessary to remind smokers of their imminent demise. As Kurt Vonnegut once wrote, "The real reason why people still smoke, is that smoking is a fairly certain and fairly socially acceptable way of killing yourself."

Yes; that's right. We smokers knowingly and gladly trade minutes, even hours off of our lives each time we suck down a warm, soothing puff of tobacco smoke. The Truth teenagers, for all their self-righteous well meaning, are preaching to the Bishops.

The worst product of this smarmy ad campaign is the coughing. There is nothing in this green world more mind numbingly irritating as a group of snotty children purposefully hacking and coughing because you happen to be smoking a cigarette. "Yeah, the car exhaust gets to me too" I usually say to them. I doubt they get it. If I put my cigarette out on their forehead, maybe they would get it. No; that would be bad. Why can't someone run an add campaign for "Mind your own business kid!"

Smoking Is Cooler than Protesting It

It is my dumb luck to live in a society that empowers children and forbids their beating in public. For now I will have to be content with the small yet surviving generational underbelly of maladapted and dissolutioned kids. Their kind can still be seen, puffing away on certain death in an attempt to progress their image far beyond their physical years.

A flyer once graced the bulletin boards of my college hallways. Underneath a picture of John Travolta cunningly blowing cigarette smoke it read "No matter how bad it is for you, smoking will always make you look cool."

Yeah.

How Can Teen Smoking Be Reduced and Prevented?

Ten Things Quitters Should Avoid

Terry Martin

Many people try to quit smoking without any clear idea how difficult the process can be and fail in their attempt because of unforeseen hurdles. In this selection, Terry Martin points out the many "don'ts" aspiring nonsmokers should take into consideration. From patience to good nutrition, smokers need to focus on every aspect of their personality and their lives. Terry Martin writes for About.com.

We all want this quit to be *the* quit—the one that lasts us a lifetime. We're looking for permanent freedom from nicotine addiction. Let's take a look at some of the things you should avoid when quitting tobacco. Build a strong quit program by educating yourself about the process!

Don't be impatient. The natural tendency is to quit smoking and expect to be done with it within a month. Smoking cessation doesn't work that way, however. When you quit smoking, you are letting go of a habit that you've had for many years, if not all of your adult life. It's only fair to expect that breaking all of the old associations that tied you to smoking will take some time. Sit back, relax, and put some time between you and that last smoke you had. Have patience with yourself, and with the process.

Don't worry about forever. It can be overwhelming to think you'll never smoke another cigarette, so don't. Don't focus on forever, focus on the day you have in front of you. This is where your power is, and always will be. You can't do a thing about yesterday or tomorrow, but you sure can control today, If you find your mind wandering ahead or back, pull yourself out of it by focusing on the present.

Terry Martin, "10 Things to Avoid When You Quit Smoking," About.com, May 29, 2007. Reproduced by permission.

Thinking Positively Is Key

Don't be negative. It's been said that the average person has approximately 66,000 thoughts in a given day, and that two-thirds of them are negative. We can be so hard on ourselves! Don't beat yourself up for things you can't change, such as the years you spent smoking. And don't look at past quit attempts as failures. Learn from the experiences you've had and move on. Think about all of the positive changes you're creating in your life by quitting tobacco.

Successful long-term cessation *always* starts in the mind. Keep your eye on the prize and develop an attitude of gratitude. We have a way of believing what we tell ourselves over and over, so don't feed yourself negatives. Affirm the changes you are working to create in your life, and action will follow more easily.

Don't neglect yourself. This is a time when you should be taking extra care to make sure all of your needs are being met. The following guidelines will help you weather withdrawal more comfortably:

- *Eat a well-balanced diet.* Your body needs good quality fuel now more than ever as it works to flush the toxins out of your system.

- *Get more rest.* Chances are you'll feel extra fatigue for a few weeks. Don't fight it. Sleep more if you can.

- *Drink water.* Water is a great quit aid. It helps you detox more quickly, works well as a craving-buster, and by keeping yourself hydrated, you'll feel better overall.

- *Exercise daily.* Walking is a wonderful way to get exercise. It's a good, low impact aerobic workout, and it works well to keep cravings in check. Take a few 15-minute walks every day and see if it improves your spirits.

- *Take a daily multi-vitamin.* Your body can use the extra boost a vitamin provides for the duration of withdrawal from nicotine. Cigarettes deplete so many nutrients. A daily multi-vitamin may help you regain your energy more quickly.

Withdrawal isn't a pain-free experience, but it is survivable, and it is certainly short-lived. Always keep in mind the fact that *withdrawal from nicotine is a temporary condition.*

Alcohol and Tobacco Go Hand-in-Hand

Don't drink. I probably don't need to tell you that alcohol and tobacco go hand-in-hand. New quitters are tender. Putting yourself into a social setting where you're tempted to drink too soon after quitting can be dangerous. Don't rush it. The time will come when you can have a drink without it triggering the urge to smoke, but don't expect that to be within the first month, or perhaps even the first few months.

We're all a little different in how we go through recovery, so defining a specific time frame isn't realistic. Just be aware of your own situation. If you have an engagement coming up that involves drinking and you feel nervous about that, it might be best to postpone until you're feeling stronger. If that's not an option, have a plan in place for how you'll manage the event smoke free.

Will you be able to excuse yourself to step out for some fresh air? Can you request that people don't smoke around you?

However you decide to handle the situation, don't be shy about it. This is your life we're talking about here, and quitting tobacco has to be a top priority for awhile. Whatever you need to do to maintain your quit, you should do. Period! Remember, life won't always be this way—it will return to normal eventually.

Don't overdo. We've talked about taking care not to neglect your physical health. Your emotional well-being is every bit as important. Stress can build if you're not careful, and before you know it, you re fighting a strong urge to smoke. Early cessation creates its own tension, let alone all of the other stresses that come and go in our busy daily lives. Make sure you don't let yourself get run down to the point of exhaustion, and that you take time *every single day* to destress with an activity that you enjoy. Whether it's time alone with a good book, a hot bath, or working on a hobby, make sure you incorporate some time just for you.

Fatigue and stress are big triggers to smoke, and it can be a quick jump to feeling that you need a cigarette to cope. Plan *ahead of time* how you'll keep yourself out of those danger zones.

Not Everything Will Go Smoothly

Don't take yourself too seriously. You will have bad days. Expect and accept that. Such is cessation, and such is life. On those off days, make a vow to put yourself on ignore! Sometimes the best thing we can do is to get out of our own way. Our minds can make a small issue big, and make a drama out of every little thing if our moods are out of whack. When you have a bad day, use it as an excuse to pamper yourself excessively. Be good to yourself and put your thoughts on hold. Decide to wait and see what tomorrow will bring. Nine times out of ten you'll wake up feeling 100 percent better the next day. And when you do, you'll be grateful to still be smoke free.

Don't be afraid to ask for help. Statistics show that people who quit with a healthy support system in place have a much higher rate of success over time. If you don't have people around you who are supportive, and even if you do, add some online support to your quit program. . . . There is nothing better than bending the ear of a person who knows *exactly* what you are going through. Getting help from people who have 'been there and done that' is worth its weight in gold.

Don't believe that you can have "just one." There is no such thing. It doesn't work with Lays potato chips, and it sure doesn't work with cigarettes. Smoke one cigarette, and you run a very high risk of being back to a pack a day quicker than you can imagine. Don't fall for faulty thinking. *A relapse* always *begins in the mind.* If you recognize unhealthy thoughts of smoking cropping up, it's time to renew your resolve.

Don't forget. You quit smoking for a reason. Probably several. Don't let time and distance from the habit cloud your thinking. Keep your memory green by reviewing your reasons often. They will never be less true as time goes by, but they can feel less critical if you're not careful.

Cessation is a journey. Take it one simple day at a time, and you'll find that what started out as a difficult task soon enough becomes an enjoyable challenge.

Parents Are the Best Prevention

Barbara P. Homeier and Neil Izenberg

In this article Barbara Homeier and Neil Izenberg come to the conclusion that the best influence against teen smoking is parental guidance. They show ways for parents to help prevent their kids from picking up the habit, and offer advice on how to get teenagers off cigarettes once they have started. Homeier is a doctor at Alfred I. Du Pont Hospital for Children in Wilmington, Delaware. Izenberg is professor of pediatrics at Jefferson Medical College in Philadelphia, Pennsylvania.

The health risks of tobacco are well known, yet the rates of smoking and the use of chewing tobacco continue to grow. Many people are picking up these habits when they are young—in fact, 90% of all adult smokers started when they were kids. And each day, more than 4,400 kids become regular smokers.

So it's important to make sure your child understands the dangers that go along with using tobacco. Smoking is the leading cause of preventable deaths in the United States. It can cause cancer, heart disease, or lung disease. Chewing tobacco (smokeless or spit tobacco) can lead to nicotine addiction, oral cancer, gum disease, and an increased risk of cardiovascular disease, including heart attacks.

If you arm your child with information about the risks of smoking and chewing tobacco, and establish clear rules and your reasons for them, you can help prevent your child from picking up those unhealthy habits. If your child is already using tobacco, there are warning signs that can clue you in and constructive ways to help your child quit.

The Facts About Tobacco

One of the major problems with smoking and chewing tobacco has to do with the chemical *nicotine*. A person can get addicted to nicotine within days of a first encounter with it. In fact, the nicotine in tobacco can be as addictive as cocaine or heroine. Nicotine affects a person's mood as well as the heart, lungs, stomach, and nervous system.

And there are other health risks. Short-term effects of smoking include coughing and throat irritation. Over time, more serious conditions may develop, including increases in heart rate and blood pressure. Smoking also leads to bronchitis and emphysema.

Finally, numerous studies indicate that young smokers are more likely to experiment with marijuana, cocaine, heroin, or other illicit drugs.

Preventing Your Child from Picking Up the Habit

Kids tend to be drawn to smoking and chewing tobacco for any number of reasons—to look cool, act older, lose weight, win cool merchandise, seem tough, or feel independent. But you can combat those draws and keep your child from trying—and getting addicted to—tobacco.

If you establish a good foundation of communication with your child early, it will be much easier later on to work through tricky issues like tobacco use. Here are a few guidelines to keep in mind:

- Discuss other sensitive topics in a way that doesn't make your child fear punishment or judgment.

- Emphasize what your child does right rather than wrong. Self-confidence is your child's best protection against peer pressure.

- Encourage your child to get involved in activities that prohibit smoking, such as sports.

- Show your child that you value his or her opinions and ideas.

- When it comes to the dangers of tobacco use, it's important to keep talking to your child about it over the years. Even the youngest child can understand that smoking is bad for the body.

- Ask your child what he or she finds appealing—or unappealing—about smoking. Be a patient listener.

- Read, watch television, and go to the movies with your child. Compare media images with what happens in reality.

- Discuss ways to respond to peer pressure to smoke. Your child may feel confident simply saying "no." But also offer your child alternative responses such as "It will make my clothes and breath smell bad" or "I hate the way it makes me look."

- Encourage your child to walk away from friends who don't recognize or respect his or her reasons for not smoking.

- Explain how much smoking governs the daily life of kids who start doing it. How do they afford the cigarettes? How do they have money to pay for other things they want? How does it affect their friendships?

- Establish firm rules that exclude smoking and chewing tobacco from your house and explain why: Smokers smell bad, look bad, and feel bad, and it's bad for everyone's health.

Signs That Your Child May Have Started Smoking

If you smell smoke on your child's clothing, try not to overreact. Ask your child about it first. It may mean your child has been hanging around with friends who smoke or that your child has simply tried a cigarette. Many kids do try a cigarette at one time or another but don't go on to become regular smokers.

Some additional signs of tobacco use include:

- coughing

- throat irritation

- hoarseness

- bad breath

- decreased athletic performance

- greater susceptibility to colds

- stained teeth and clothing (which also can be signs of chewing tobacco use)

- shortness of breath

What to Do If Your Child Already Smokes

Sometimes even the best foundation isn't enough to stop a child from experimenting with tobacco. Although it may be tempting to get angry, it might be more productive to focus on communicating with your child. Here are some tips that may help:

- Resist lecturing or turning your advice into a sermon.

- Uncover what appeals to your child about smoking and talk about it honestly.

- Remind your child about the immediate downsides to smoking: less money to spend on other pursuits, shortness of breath, bad breath, yellow teeth, and smelly clothes. Many times, kids aren't able to appreciate how their current behaviors can affect their future health.

- Stick to the smoking rules you've set up. And don't let your child smoke at home to keep him or her at home or to keep the peace.

- If your child says, "I can quit any time I want," ask him or her to show you by quitting cold turkey for a week.

- Don't nag your child to quit. Ultimately, the decision is your child's—focus on helping your child to make a wise one.

- Help your child develop a quitting plan and offer information and resources.

- Reinforce your child's decision to quit with praise.

- Stress the natural rewards that come with quitting: freedom from addiction, improved fitness, better athletic performance, and improved appearance.

- Encourage a meeting with your child's doctor, who can be supportive emotionally and may have treatment plans.

If You Smoke

Kids are quick to observe any contradiction between what their parents say and what they do. Despite what you might think, most kids say that the adult whom they most want to be like when they grow up is a parent.

If you're a smoker:

- First, admit to your child that you made a mistake by starting to smoke and that if you had it to do over again, you'd never start.

- Second, quit. It's not simple by any means. It may take several attempts and the extra help of a program or support group. But your child will be encouraged as he or she sees you overcome your addiction to tobacco.

Curbing Teen Smoking

Dave Hitt

This humorous essay targets antismoking legislation and anti-smoking campaigns. If we want to curb teen smoking, Dave Hitt claims, we have to make it look less desirable. One way to accomplish this, he suggests, is turning boring celebrities into smoking advocates. Only if we can convince children that only undesirable people are smoking, will teen smoking decline. Dave Hitt is the author of the Hittman Chronicle, *an online journal.*

State and Federal governments are eagerly passing anti-tobacco legislation. They claim noble motives; they're doing it to "Protect The Children." (When they use that phrase you can actually hear the capital letters.) They brush off the fact that it will transfer huge amounts of money from smokers' pockets into their own as an unfortunate side effect.

Teen smoking can only be curbed by addressing the real reason teens smoke: Smoking is cool. It is so cool that non-smoking teens who hang around smoking teens are affected by second hand coolness. Everything the government is doing, from condemning smoking to raising taxes to enforcing age limits makes smoking more cool, not less.

The only way to reduce teen smoking is to make it less cool. Congress, the least cool people on the planet, need to understand cool before they can remove it from cigarettes.

Understanding Cool Is Key

Some things are cool for no apparent reason. Sunglasses are cool, and Wayfarer sunglasses are the coolest because, well, because they are. But most cool things share three common characteristics: they're dangerous, they annoy parents, author-

Dave Hitt, "The Only Way to Curb Teen Smoking," *The Hittman Chronicle*, April 1999. www.davehitt.com. Reproduced by permission.

ity figures and busybodies, and they are done/used/worn by cool people. Smoking shares every one of these traits, and will remain cool until each factor is reduced or eliminated.

Everyone knows smoking is dangerous. Removing just a little of the danger will remove much of the cool. When we teach kids that smoking causes cancer, heart desease, and emphysema, only the bravest (coolest) kids dare to smoke. We can remove much of the daring-do by reporting the health effects more accurately. Smoking doesn't cause these diseases, it simply increases the risk of getting them. Sure, it increases the risk substantially, but there's no guarantee that smoking will lead to a slow, painful death. Everyone knows someone who smoked two packs a day and lived to a ripe old age. Old age is very uncool among teenagers. So instead of teaching that smoking causes these diseases, let's be more accurate and say smoking increases your risk of getting them.

Removing the coolness factor of annoying parents, authority figures, and busybodies will be more difficult.

Risks and Bans Make Smoking Cool

Parents, talking to your kids about the dangers of smoking is almost an invitation to light up. Your disapproval makes it cool. Fortunately, there are other methods of discouraging your kids from starting or encouraging them to quit.

Every teenager knows their parents were never cool, so if you used to smoke in your teens tell your kids about it as often as possible. If you still smoke, do it in front of your kids at every opportunity, preferably while listening to oldies tunes they hate. If you really want to make your kids fling their smokes away in disgust, dance. In one recent study 80% of the teenage smokers tested quit immediately after a single exposure to the sight of their parents smoking and dancing The Swim to [Pop Song] *Woolly Bully*. (Note: Do not try to enhance the effect by wearing bellbottoms, as they are now, frighteningly, considered cool among teens.)

Authority figures should just shut up about the subject. It's hard to imagine anyone less cool than former FDA [Food and Drug Administration] chief David Kessler, his eyes full of righteous indignation and magnified by the world's dorkyest looking coke-bottle glasses. Every time he made a public statement about tobacco thousands of kids started smoking in a desperate attempt to be as unlike him [as] possible.

Busybodies present a special challenge. Normal people achieve self-assurance by accomplishing things. Busybodies can only feel important by looking down on others. Any attempt to discourage their interference in other people's lives is doomed to fail. Without others to look down on, click their tongues at, and inspire their angry letters to Congress their lives would have no meaning.

Busybodies Are the Source of Evil

We can't stop them, but perhaps we can change the target of their wrath. Using commercials, emotional appeals, distorted and fabricated statistics, gross photographs, and anything else except real facts (which they despise and ignore) let's convince them that people who don't recognize the rights of animals are even more evil than smokers. Animal rights activists are always overjoyed to find others silly enough to join their cause. Their twisted statistics are even goofier than those used by anti-tobacco nannies. There are far more carnivores than smokers, giving the busybodies more people to despise. As an added bonus, if they do it right and become vegetarians, there will be more burgers for the rest of us.

The last, most important and most difficult trait to deal with is cool people smoking. We can't stop them, but we can counter it by showing un-cool people smoking. We should start with the aforementioned David Kessler. Just as his preaching caused kids to start smoking, watching him light up a Marlboro would cause thousands of kids to quit immediately. Tens of thousands would quit if they saw Michael Bolton [singer] with a cigarette. And we could make every teenager in the country gag with disgust at the thought of smoking if we could just get one particular celebrity to endorse the habit. It would be difficult, as he considers himself a fitness guru, but perhaps we could convince him to do it for the kids:

"Hi, I'm Richard Simmons [fitness expert], and smoking made me the man I am today!"

Youth Tobacco Cessation

Micah H. Milton

In this selection Micah Milton writes about what smokers who want to quit can do to be successful. Providing extensive background material, this text explains the different intervention strategies and programs, and encourages people to find the best way for them to stop using tobacco. Micah Milton is a scientist at the Centers for Disease Control and Prevention.

More than 80% of adult tobacco users in the United States began using tobacco regularly before age 18. The prevalence of tobacco use is now higher among teenagers and young adults than among other adult populations. However, the prevalence of quitting (i.e., the percentage of those who have ever smoked who are now former smokers) also is lower among these younger age groups. Studies indicate that most teenaged and young adult smokers want to quit and try to do so, but few succeed. Many of these young smokers will eventually die from a smoking-related disease. Although many people are aware that adult smokers are more likely to have heart disease, cancer, and emphysema, many negative health consequences also occur among youth.

Examples of negative health consequences for youth who smoke include the following:

- Smoking hurts young people's physical fitness in terms of both performance and endurance, including those trained in competitive running.

- Smoking can hamper the rate of lung growth and the level of maximum lung function among youth.

Micah H. Milton, "What You Should Know About Tobacco-Use Cessation," *Youth Tobacco Cessation: A Guide for Making Informed Decisions*, 2004. Information obtained from the Centers for Disease Control (www.cdc.gov).

- The resting heart rates of young adult smokers are 2–3 beats per minute faster than those of nonsmokers.

- Regular smoking is responsible for cough and increased frequency and severity of respiratory illnesses.

- The younger a person starts smoking, the more likely he is to become strongly addicted to nicotine. Most young people who smoke regularly continue to smoke throughout adulthood, leading to long-term health consequences.

- Teenagers who smoke are 3 times more likely than nonsmokers to use alcohol, 8 times more likely to use marijuana, and 22 times more likely to use cocaine. Smoking is associated with several other risk behaviors, such as fighting and engaging in unprotected sex.

- High school seniors who are regular smokers and who began smoking by grade 9 are 2.4 times more likely than their nonsmoking peers to report poorer overall health; 2.4–2.7 times more likely to report cough with phlegm or blood, shortness of breath when not exercising, and wheezing or gasping; and 3.0 times more likely to have seen a doctor or other health professional for an emotional or psychological complaint.

- Smoking may be a marker for underlying mental health problems, such as depression, among adolescents.

The Progression of Youth Tobacco Use

The immediate impetus to experiment with tobacco is often social, prompted by friends, family members, or other role models who smoke. However, various other factors—some of which may make certain youth more susceptible to addiction and long-term use—contribute to initiation and progression toward regular tobacco use. . . .

The process by which a person moves from experimenting with tobacco to becoming a regular user can include the following five stages.

- The *preparatory stage*, when a person's knowledge, beliefs, and expectations about tobacco use are formed.

- The *initial/trying stage*, when a person tries the first few cigarettes.

- The *experimentation stage*, which is a period of repeat, irregular use that may occur only in specific situations over a variable time.

- *Regular tobacco use*, when a routine pattern of use has developed. For youth, this may mean using tobacco every weekend or at certain times of the day.

- *Nicotine addiction*, which is regular tobacco use, usually daily, with an internally regulated need for nicotine.

Tobacco Prevalence

Tobacco use is pervasive among youth across North America. In Canada, 22% of teenagers aged 15–19 reported in 2002 that they were current smokers, down from 28% in 1999. In the United States, 21.9% of high school students reported in 2003 that they had smoked cigarettes in the previous month. . . . Tobacco use among U.S. youth declined slowly during the 1980s, increased rapidly during the early 1990s, and then declined significantly during 1997–2003.

Nicotine Dependence

Nicotine is an addictive drug in tobacco that people are likely to begin using in adolescence. People who begin using tobacco at an early age are more likely to develop more severe levels of nicotine addiction than those who begin when they are older. Like other drug addictions, nicotine dependence is a chronic condition with the potential for relapse throughout one's life.

Typically, people become addicted to nicotine when they increase the frequency of tobacco use. However, dependence may begin very early for some people.

Although most youth do not become nicotine dependent until after 2–3 years of use, addiction can occur after smoking as few as 100 cigarettes. Studies have shown that some young people report symptoms of dependence within the first weeks, even with very irregular or sporadic use. Other studies have reported less evidence for nicotine addiction among youth, citing the irregular patterns of use and higher spontaneous quit rates as evidence that addiction is not common among this population. Some adolescent tobacco users probably are dependent and may therefore suffer symptoms of physical and/or psychological withdrawal when attempting to quit.

Youth's Desire to Quit and Quit Attempts

Many young people report a desire to quit and previous attempts at quitting. Of current smokers aged 15–19 in Canada, 64% reported one or more quit attempts in the 12 months before being surveyed. In the United States, approximately 60% of current smokers in high school and middle school reported one or more quit attempts in the year before being surveyed.

Although many youth think about and attempt to quit tobacco, many are unaware of or unable to access cessation services. Also, many youth do not think that quitting tobacco is difficult enough to warrant professional assistance, and they report not having much interest in participating in such interventions. Others may not access interventions or services that do not appear to address their particular needs or concerns. For these reasons, recruitment strategies ... should be a critical component of your intervention plan.

The immediate need for effective cessation support has been clearly expressed, both by youth and by people who work with them. In response, efforts have increased recently to improve our understanding of how to provide effective cessation interventions to youth. This demand was the primary motivation for developing this publication.

National Goals for Reducing Youth Tobacco Use

Healthy People 2010 established national targets for reducing tobacco use and increasing quit attempts by youth in the United States. Specific objectives include the following:

- Reduce the use of tobacco products by youth in the past month from 40% to 21%.

- Reduce cigarette smoking by youth in the past month from 35% to 16%.

- Increase the proportion of regular smokers in grades 9–12 who have made a quit attempt from 61% to 84%.

The Centers for Disease Control and Prevention (CDC) recommends that one of the major goals of any tobacco control program should be to promote quitting among both young people and adults. CDC also recommends that comprehensive school health programs should include efforts to help students and school staff members quit.

Guidelines for Youth Tobacco-Use Cessation

Recommendations for "best practices" typically are based on a review of data, usually from the scientific literature, on such topics as health care services or policies. The review is designed to show the effectiveness of specific practices. For example, the recommendations in the U.S. Public Health Service's (PHS's) *Treating Tobacco Use and Dependence: Clinical Practice Guideline*, were developed from an initial review of about 6,000 articles, of which 180 were deemed appropriate to the evidence base for making recommendations.

In the area of youth tobacco-use cessation, fewer than 80 studies had been published in scientific journals as of spring

2001. Variations in study aims and intervention content, format, focus, and context made comparisons among these studies difficult. Many studies had small sample sizes, used study designs that did not include comparison groups, or did not report enough information to describe the intervention. These limitations reduced the ability to prove evidence of effectiveness. Thus, making recommendations from the published literature was not possible.

The "Better Practices" Model

Despite the lack of evidence-based interventions, recommendations on how to help youth quit using tobacco are needed now. To address this need, a new approach developed by the Canadian Tobacco Control Research Initiative (CTCRI) was used to review the existing evidence and try to develop practical guidelines. This "better practices" model is based on the idea that successful solutions to complex problems must draw from both science and experience. The resulting guidelines also take into account the specific needs of a given population and situation and the resources available to address those needs.

With this in mind, the special advisory panel that helped develop this publication outlined guidelines on what issues should be considered when developing youth tobacco-use cessation interventions. As the evidence base continues to expand, we should eventually be able to identify specific best practices for youth. In the meantime, the advice provided in this publication can guide you in deciding whether to implement a youth tobacco-use cessation intervention and in choosing and implementing appropriate interventions. All interventions must be monitored and rigorously evaluated . . . to advance knowledge in this area.

Apply Your Experience

Another approach is to apply past experience working with youth in clinical practice, tobacco prevention activities, and interventions that address other risk behaviors or conditions. Information also can be drawn from the growing knowledge about what components of comprehensive tobacco control programs are most critical (e.g., prevention policies and interventions, secondhand smoke protections, cessation interventions, changes in public attitudes toward tobacco use).

One example of how these types of peripheral knowledge can support cessation efforts can be found in counter-marketing. Research suggests that youth are particularly susceptible to tobacco advertising and promotions. If youth are similarly influenced by counter-marketing, then learning about the strategies and tactics that the tobacco industry uses to target them may stimulate young smokers' interest in tobacco-use cessation and empower them to reject the tobacco industry's marketing efforts.

Applying Adult Interventions to Youth

Because of the lack of best practices for youth tobacco-use cessation interventions, we should consider the efforts that have been effective in adult cessation and determine whether such practices could be effective, appropriate, and adaptable to meet the needs of young tobacco users wanting to quit. In 2000, the PHS published *Treating Tobacco Use and Dependence: Clinical Practice Guideline*, which provides evidence-based recommendations to increase the likelihood of successful tobacco-use cessation for adults who access health care systems.

Although evidence was lacking on what works for adolescent patients, the PHS recommended the following clinician actions on the basis of expert opinion:

- Clinicians should screen pediatric and adolescent patients and their parents for tobacco use and provide a strong message regarding the importance of totally abstaining from tobacco use.

- Counseling and behavioral interventions shown to be effective with adults should be considered for use with children and adolescents. The content of these interventions should be modified to be developmentally appropriate.

- When treating adolescents, clinicians may consider prescriptions for bupropion sustained-release or nicotine replacement therapy when there is evidence of nicotine dependence and desire to quit tobacco use.

- Clinicians in a pediatric setting should offer tobacco-use cessation advice and interventions to parents to limit children's exposure to secondhand smoke.

Another approach is to apply the lessons learned about what works with adults as a starting point for youth tobacco-use cessation strategies. The PHS clinical practice recommendations for adults indicate the following:

- Tobacco dependence is a chronic condition that often requires repeated intervention.

- If willing to quit, tobacco users should have access to effective treatments. If unwilling, tobacco users should be provided with brief interventions to increase their motivation to quit.

- A strong dose-response relationship exists between the intensity of tobacco-use cessation counseling and its effectiveness.

- Offering social support (both within and outside the treatment setting) and teaching problem-solving skills show promise for helping tobacco users quit.

- Pharmacotherapies are available and can be used in the absence of contraindications for people experiencing symptoms of nicotine withdrawal. However, youth are less likely to show signs of physical withdrawal than adults, and pharmacotherapies have not been shown to be effective among adolescents.

A Note of Caution

Intervention providers should use caution when adapting adult interventions for youth, and they should evaluate their efforts carefully. What works for one population may not work for another. What works in one setting (e.g., a health care visit) may not work in another (e.g., a school). For example, providers have learned from working with adults that providing social support through group counseling is an effective aid to cessation efforts. However, people who work with youth on other sensitive issues, such as substance use and sexual behavior, know that privacy concerns can make group interventions inappropriate for this population. By understanding the needs and concerns of the youth you serve, you will be able to select the intervention components that best meet their needs.

The characteristics of youth and the context of their lives are unique and significantly contribute to their tobacco use and cessation behaviors. For example, youth typically have more variable patterns of tobacco use than adults. Many young people underestimate the addictiveness of tobacco and the effect of tobacco use on their health. In fact, the actual idea of "cessation" is often different for youth than it is for adults.

Youth who use tobacco may be reluctant to identify themselves as "smokers" or "tobacco users," and subsequently, their commitments to "quitting" may be equally variable. For these reasons, we may not be able to draw conclusions about what works for youth tobacco-use cessation on the basis of what works for adults.

A Comprehensive Approach to Tobacco Control

Overcoming tobacco dependence, like with any addiction, is not a single event. It is a complex and continuous process mitigated by an array of physical, social, and psychological factors. Many factors can prompt people to begin using tobacco, and many variables can prompt them to quit. A single intervention or activity is unlikely to be effective and suitable for every person in the population you serve.

For this reason, CDC recommends that all tobacco control programs be comprehensive. Comprehensive programs can create the synergy and supportive environment needed to help youth quit. One organization is unlikely to be able to provide every component for a comprehensive program. However, different organizations can coordinate their efforts to achieve comprehensive programs in their communities.

A comprehensive tobacco control program should include the following components.

- Tobacco-use prevention efforts that jointly involve education, community activities, and counter-marketing.

- Legislative and policy efforts to limit tobacco use, stop tobacco advertising and promotions, promote clean indoor air, restrict youth access to tobacco, and increase the cost of tobacco through taxation.

- Enforcement of existing laws and policies.

- Cessation interventions for both adults and youth.

- Interventions to prevent or reduce the burden of chronic diseases related to tobacco use.

- Surveillance and evaluation to improve knowledge about best practices in tobacco control.

- Tobacco control efforts that operate at multiple levels (i.e., state or province, community, and school).

- Administrative and managerial activities that coordinate tobacco control efforts at the community level and at state, province, or other larger jurisdiction levels.

Incorporating Youth Interventions into Comprehensive Programs

The decision about whether to implement a cessation intervention for youth is complicated and may be influenced by many factors. The impetus for developing such an intervention can come from different sources (e.g., the criminal justice system, state agencies, community groups, youth). Decisions should be made only after taking into account the services currently offered in your area, along with how your new services will be supported and integrated.

When considering whether to offer a cessation intervention for youth, first determine whether a comprehensive tobacco control program already exists in your area. If it does, assess how your intervention will enhance these efforts. If a comprehensive program does not exist, assess what tobacco interventions should be created or strengthened and what contribution your intervention can offer toward a more comprehensive approach. . . .

The Importance of Environmental Factors

Strong voluntary and regulatory policies that deter tobacco use and protect youth from secondhand smoke are critical to helping youth quit. Increases in taxes on tobacco, which raise the overall cost, significantly reduce tobacco use by youth. Smoke-free policies in public places make tobacco use less socially acceptable which also may help to prevent and reduce tobacco use by youth. In communities where such measures are not in place, people interested in youth tobacco-use cessation should actively campaign for policy changes that can benefit all community members.

Counter-advertising also can play a significant role in reducing tobacco use by youth. As noted previously, youth are very susceptible to the influence of tobacco industry advertisements. Mass media campaigns can counter that effect and help create an environment in which tobacco use is less acceptable, thereby increasing the motivation to quit. Even when counter-advertising is aimed at preventing tobacco use among youth, it may benefit youth tobacco-use cessation by increasing interest in quitting.

If cessation resources already exist for adults, they could be expanded to include interventions for youth. A comprehensive tobacco control program that includes cessation interventions for both adults and youth and links them to existing cessation resources (e.g., quitlines) could be established.

Another important factor is the environment in which an intervention is delivered. For example, a school-based intervention may lose credibility if teachers are seen using tobacco on school grounds (whether inside or outside a building). To counter this effect, smoke-free school policies should be established and enforced, as recommended by CDC.

Schools Can Help Students Fight Tobacco

Meg Gallogly

Not only parents can make a difference when it comes to teenage smoking—schools and teachers can also help prevent tobacco use, or offer help when students want to quit. In this article Meg Gallogly suggests a variety of methods that allow teachers and administrators to curb teen smoking and reduce tobacco addiction significantly. Meg Gallogly is an anti-tobacco activist.

Schools are in a uniquely powerful position to play a major role in reducing the serious problem of smoking and other tobacco use by kids. Children spend almost a third of their waking time in school, or about 135 hours per month—and much of the peer pressure kids feel regarding whether or not to smoke occurs in school. Moreover, the vast majority of all smokers begin before leaving high school. A national survey in 2003 found that 10.2 percent of eighth graders, 16.7 percent of tenth graders, and 24.4 percent of twelfth graders had smoked in the past month. Unfortunately, this problem begins long before high school, or even junior high. Very little data about smoking is regularly collected for kids under 12, but the peak years for first trying to smoke appear to be in the sixth and seventh grades, or between the ages of 11 and 12, with a considerable number starting even earlier. For example, in a nationwide *Monitoring the Future* survey, thirteen percent of eighth grade students reported having first smoked by the fifth grade (ages 10 and 11), and 28 percent have tried smoking by the eighth grade. If these trends are not changed, more than five million kids under age 18 alive today will ultimately die prematurely from smoking.

Meg Gallogly, "How Schools Can Help Students Stay Tobacco-Free," *Campaign for Tobacco-Free Kids* (www.tobaccofreekids.org), January 15, 2004. Reproduced by permission.

Smoking and other tobacco use also causes a number of immediate, sometimes irreversible, health effects and risks that can seriously damage kids' health well before they leave school or reach adulthood. At the same time, symptoms of serious addiction that can lead to years of dependent use can appear within weeks, or even days after occasional smoking begins. While only three percent of daily smokers in high school think that they'll still be smoking in five years, more than 60 percent are still regular daily smokers seven to nine years later. Smoking may also be a "gateway" to illegal drug use. Adolescent smoking usually precedes illegal drug use, and the earlier a child experiments with tobacco the more likely he or she is to use marijuana, cocaine, heroin, and other illicit drugs.

The Role of Schools in Reducing Youth Smoking and Other Tobacco Use

For schools to effectively prevent and reduce youth smoking among their students, they must create an environment that encourages anti-smoking beliefs and behaviors. . . .

- *Forbid smoking by students, staff, and visitors on all school grounds and at all school-sponsored events.* School smoke-free policies that are clearly and consistently communicated, applied, and enforced reduce smoking among students. While just making sure that no kids smoke at school is helpful, also prohibiting smoking by teachers, other school staff, and visitors sends a much more powerful and constructive anti-smoking message. At the very least, any tobacco use by teachers, staff, or others on school grounds or at school activities should be completely invisible to students. Simply adopting firm smoke-free policies for all school properties and events will have a strong positive impact, but these policies are even more effective when they are accompanied by prevention and cessation education. Many schools are already required to prohibit smoking because the Federal Pro Children Act of 1994 prohibits smoking in facilities that regularly provide certain Federally funded children's services.

• *Provide comprehensive tobacco prevention education.* School-based education programs to prevent and reduce youth smoking work, but they have to be done right. To work best, such programs should not focus on only one aspect of smoking, such as the short- and long-term negative health effects but should also address social acceptability, social influences, negative social consequences from tobacco use, peer norms and peer pressure, resistance and refusal skills, and media literacy as it relates to tobacco marketing and advertising. In addition, it is not enough to offer anti-smoking education only in middle school or early high school. Students should receive this instruction and guidance, in one form or another, throughout their educational experience. Effective youth tobacco prevention programs are grade and age sensitive, with the most intense instruction in middle school and reinforcement throughout high school.

• *Provide program-specific training for teachers.* When teachers are trained to properly deliver tobacco prevention curriculum, the success of the overall program is greatly improved. Effective training should include a review of curriculum content, modeling of program activities by skilled trainers, and the opportunity for teachers to practice implementing program activities.

Parents and Families Need to Join the Prevention Effort

• *Involve parents and families in school efforts to prevent tobacco use.* Families have an enormous influence on students' smoking perceptions and attitudes, and family members should be involved in school anti-smoking efforts as much as possible. Programs that include interactive homework assignments that educate and involve parents and other family members not only increase family discussions on this important topic but can lead to better home policies about tobacco use and even encourage adult smokers to try to quit.

- *Offer interactive anti-smoking projects for students.* To reinforce the school's anti-smoking policies, and enliven its related programs, schools should offer students opportunities to work on projects to reduce the pro-smoking influences in their communities. For example, students could do a survey of stores near their school that advertise and sell tobacco products, and then write letters to the store owners urging them to reduce or eliminate their externally visible tobacco-product ads and put all their tobacco products behind the counter. Similarly, students could start a letter-writing campaign to encourage magazines available in the school library to stop running any tobacco-product advertisements. The Campaign for Tobacco-Free Kids' Kick Butts Day activity guide describes additional anti-smoking projects for students that can be done independently or as part of Kick Butts Day each year.

- *Help tobacco-using students and staff quit.* Efforts to reduce smoking among school kids cannot solely focus on preventing kids from starting. Too many kids already smoke, and these kids need help quitting. In fact, 61 percent of high school smokers report that they want to quit smoking. Likewise, while the vast majority of adult smokers want to quit, a CDC [Centers for Disease Control and Prevention] study found that only about six percent were able to quit for a month or longer. Schools can improve these quitting percentages by providing effective cessation assistance to their smoking students and staff. If school-run cessation programs are not possible, schools can still provide students and staff with information on how to quit and on how to link up with community-based cessation programs—or even bring program representatives to the schools. If there is a shortage of available cessation programs, schools can also play an important role in developing new ones, in conjunction with community health, youth, and other volunteer organizations. In any such efforts, schools should be mindful of the fact that successful cessation approaches differ for kids and adults. Cessation programs for adolescents, for example, should focus more on immediate consequences, offer specific attainable goals and use contracts that include rewards.

Funding from Big Tobacco Is Poisonous

- *Adopt a firm school policy of not accepting any funding, curricula, or other materials from any tobacco companies.* Tobacco companies produce and market incredibly harmful and addictive products, and they rely on kids to replace their adult customers who die or quit. Accordingly, schools should be completely off limits to tobacco companies. But the major cigarette companies have been trying to get schools to accept all sorts of assistance—such as "anti-youth-smoking" funding books, book covers, or even curricula as part of their much broader public relations and political strategies. Some schools say that the only way they can offer tobacco prevention programs and materials to their students is by taking these tobacco-company "gifts." Yet, in many cases, the schools have not even tried to find or develop alternative sources of income or assistance. In any case, accepting cigarette company funding or mate-

rials always benefits the companies a lot more than the
school, and is always a bad deal for our kids.

- *Evaluate the school's anti-smoking programs at regular
  intervals.* Schools should make sure to evaluate their
  success in implementing various smoke free policies,
  programs, and curriculum components, as well as their
  success in making a difference in the smoking patterns
  of students. This evaluation is necessary for schools to
  determine areas of their program that need improvement, as well as to demonstrate the positive effects of
  the program to students, parents, and the community—and to other schools who have not adopted tobacco prevention programs.

By taking some or all of these steps, schools can have an
enormous impact on the current and future health and well
being of their students.

Organizations to Contact

The editors have compiled the following list of organizations concerned with the issues presented in this book. The descriptions are derived from materials provided by the organizations. All have publications or information available for interested readers. The list was compiled on the date of publication of the present volume; the information provided here may change. Be aware that many organizations take several weeks or longer to respond to inquiries, so allow as much time as possible.

Agency for Healthcare Research and Quality (AHRQ)
540 Gaither Rd., Suite 2000, Rockville, MD 20850
(301) 427-1364
Web site: http://www.ahcpr.gov

The AHRQ is the leading federal agency charged with improving the quality, safety, efficiency, and effectiveness of health care for all Americans. AHRQ supports health services research that will improve the quality of health care and promote evidence-based decision making. The organization makes newsletters and reports available online.

American Cancer Society (ACS)
(866) 228-4327
Web site: www.cancer.org

The American Cancer Society (ACS) is a nationwide, community-based voluntary health organization. Headquartered in Atlanta, the ACS has state divisions and more than thirty-four hundred local offices. ACS is committed to fighting cancer through programs of research, education, patient service, advocacy, and rehabilitation. The organization publishes the periodical *Cancer*, and books on cancer-related topics.

American Lung Association (ALA)
61 Broadway, 6th Floor, New York, NY   10006
(212) 315-8700
Web site: www.lungusa.org

The mission of the ALA is to prevent lung disease and promote lung health. Founded in 1904 to fight tuberculosis, the American Lung Association today fights lung disease in all its forms, with special emphasis on asthma, tobacco control, and environmental health. It offers many school programs and publishes an e-mail newsletter.

Campaign for Tobacco-Free Kids
1400 I St., Suite 1200, Washington, DC   20005
(202) 296-5469
Web site: http://tobaccofreekids.org

The Campaign for Tobacco-Free Kids fights to reduce tobacco use and its health-related consequences in the United States and around the world. By changing public attitudes and public policies on tobacco, it works to prevent kids from smoking, help smokers quit, and protect everyone from secondhand smoke. The campaign publishes fact sheets and special reports on its Web site.

MedlinePlus
8600 Rockville Pike, Bethesda, MD   20894
Web site: http://medlineplus.gov

MedlinePlus brings together authoritative information from the U.S. National Library of Medicine (NLM), the National Institutes of Health (NIH), and other government agencies and health-related organizations. MedlinePlus offers extensive information about drugs, an illustrated medical encyclopedia, interactive patient tutorials, and current health news.

National Cancer Institute (NCI)
6116 Executive Blvd. Room 3036A
Bethesda, MD   20892-8322

(800) 4-CANCER
Web site: www.cancer.gov

The NCI, established under the National Cancer Institute Act of 1937, is the federal government's principal agency for cancer research and training. The NCI coordinates the National Cancer Program, which conducts and supports research, training, health information dissemination, and other programs with respect to the cause, diagnosis, prevention, and treatment of cancer, rehabilitation from cancer, and the continuing care of cancer patients and the families of cancer patients. The NCI publishes many articles on cancer research.

National Institute on Drug Abuse (NIDA)
6001 Executive Blvd., Bethesda, MD   20892-9561
(301) 443-1124
e-mail: information@nida.nih.gov
Web site: www.nida.nih.gov

In addition to general drug abuse prevention programs and other research efforts, NIDA also invests in public education efforts to increase awareness about the dangers of steroid abuse. NIDA publishes brochures and books on drug use for teenagers.

**Substance Abuse and Mental Health
Services Administration (SAMHSA)**
One Choke Cherry Rd., Rockville, MD   20857
Web site: www.samhsa.gov

SAMHSA has focused its mission on building resilience and facilitating recovery for people with or at risk for mental or substance use disorders. SAMHSA is gearing all of its resources—programs, policies, and grants—toward that outcome. The administration offers publications such as *Transforming Mental Health Care in America* and *Reducing Substance Abuse in America*.

World Health Organization (WHO)
525 Twenty-third St., N.W., Washington, DC   20037
(202) 974-3000 • fax: (202) 974-3663
e-mail: postmaster@paho.org
Web site: www.who.int/em

The World Health Organization is the United Nations' specialized agency for health. WHO's objective is the attainment by all peoples of the highest possible level of health. Health is defined in WHO's constitution as a state of complete physical, mental, and social well-being and not merely the absence of disease or infirmity. WHO publishes many online reports as well as books.

Bibliography

Books

American Cancer Society	*Cancer Prevention & Early Detection, Facts & Figures 2007*. Atlanta: American Cancer Society, 2007.
Rosemary Avery et al.	*Private Profits and Public Health: Does Advertising Smoking Cessation Products Encourage Smokers to Quit?* Cambridge, MA: National Bureau of Economic Research, 2006.
Allan M. Brandt	*The Cigarette Century: The Rise, Fall, and Deadly Persistence of the Product That Defined America*. New York: Basic, 2006.
Eric Burns	*The Smoke of the Gods: A Social History of Tobacco*. Philadelphia: Temple University Press, 2007.
Griffith Edwards	*Matters of Substance: Drugs—and Why Everyone's a User*. New York: Allen Lane, 2004.
Katharine M. Esson and Stephen R. Leeder	*The Millennium Development Goals and Tobacco Control: An Opportunity for Global Partnership*. Geneva, Switzerland: World Health Organization, 2004.

Jonathan Gruber and Michael Frakes	"Does Falling Smoking Lead to Rising Obesity?" *Journal of Health Economics.* Cambridge, MA: National Bureau of Economic Research, 2005.
Toshiaki Iizuka and Ginger Zhe Jin	*Drug Advertising and Health Habits.* Cambridge, MA: National Bureau of Economic Research, 2005.
Donald S. Kenkel, Dean R. Lillard, and Alan D. Mathios	*The Roles of High School Completion and GED Receipt in Smoking and Obesity.* Cambridge, MA: National Bureau of Economic Research, 2006.
Sara Markowitz	*The Effectiveness of Cigarette Regulations in Reducing Cases of Sudden Infant Death Syndrome.* Cambridge, MA: National Bureau of Economic Research, 2006.
Sara Markowitz and John Tauras	*Even for Teenagers, Money Does Not Grow on Trees: Teenage Substance Use and Budget Constraints.* Cambridge, MA: National Bureau of Economic Research, 2006.
Roddey Reid	*Globalizing Tobacco Control: Anti-Smoking Campaigns in California, France, and Japan.* Bloomington: Indiana University Press, 2005.
Robert G. Robinson et al.	*Pathways to Freedom: Winning the Fight Against Tobacco.* Atlanta: U.S. Dept. of Health and Human Services, Centers for Disease Control and Prevention, 2006.

Brian A. Rock — *Ventilation for Environmental Tobacco Smoke.* Burlington, MA: Elsevier Butterworth-Heinemann, 2006.

Jarrett Rudy — *The Freedom to Smoke: Tobacco Consumption and Identity.* Ithaca, NY: McGill-Queen's University Press, 2005.

U.S. Department of Health and Human Services — *Reducing Tobacco Use: A Report of the Surgeon General.* Atlanta: U.S. Department of Health and Human Services, Centers and Prevention, National Center for Chronic Disease Prevention and Health Promotion, Office on Smoking and Health, 2000.

Periodicals

Justin Bekelman et al. — "Effect of Industry Sponsorship on the Results of Biomedical Research," *Journal of the American Medical Association,* 2003.

Justin Bekelman et al. — "Scope and Impact of Financial Conflicts of Interest in Biomedical Research: A Systematic Review," *Journal of the American Medical Association,* 2003.

Lisa Bero et al. — "The Limits of Competing Interest Disclosures," *Tobacco Control,* 2005.

Giuseppe Biondi-Zoccai et al. — "Keeping a High Standard in Quantitative Analyses, Meta-analyses, and Systematic Reviews," *European Heart Journal,* 2007.

Campaign for Tobacco-Free Kids
"The Path to Smoking Addiction Starts at Very Young Ages," 2005. www.tobaccofreekids.org/research/factsheets/pdf/0127.pdf.

Centers for Disease Control and Prevention
"Cigarette Use Among High School Students—United States, 1991–2005," *Morbidity and Mortality Weekly Report*, 2006.

Centers for Disease Control and Prevention
"Got A Minute? Give It to Your Kid," 2006. www.cdc.gov/tobacco/tobacco/tobacco_control_programs/campaigns_events/GotaMinute_brochure.htm.

Centers for Disease Control and Prevention
"Tobacco Use, Access, and Exposure to Tobacco in Media Among Middle and High School Students—United States, 2004." *Morbidity and Mortality Weekly Report*, 2005.

Centers for Disease Control and Prevention
"Tobacco Use Among Middle and High School Students—Florida, 1988 and 1999," *Morbidity and Mortality Weekly Report*, 1999.

Centers for Disease Control and Prevention
"You(th) and Tobacco" 2006. www.cdc.gov/tobacco/youth/information_sheets/youthfax1.htm.

Centers for Disease Control and Prevention
"Youth Risk Behavior, Surveillance—United States, 1999" *Morbidity and Mortality Weekly Report*, 1999.

Simon Chapman   "The Most Important and Influential Papers in Tobacco Control: Results of an Online Poll," *Tobacco Control*, 2005.

Joseph A. DiFranza, et al.   "Tobacco Promotion and the Initiation of Tobacco Use: Assessing the Evidence for Causality," *Pediatrics*, 2006.

J. Drope et al.   "Tobacco Industry Efforts to Present Ventilation as an Alternative to Smoke-free Environments in North America," *Tobacco Control*, 2004.

Stanton Glantz   "Tobacco Money at the University of California," *American Journal of Respiratory and Critical Care Medicine*, 2005.

Barry Knishkowy and Yona Amitai   "Water-Pipe (Narghile) Smoking: An Emerging Health Risk Behavior," *Pediatrics*, 2005.

David Liebeskind, et al.   "Evidence of Publication Bias in Reporting Acute Stroke Clinical Trials," *Neurology*, 2006.

Kathleen Lohr   "Rating the Strength of Scientific Evidence: Relevance for Quality Improvement Programs," *International Journal for Quality in Health Care*, 2004.

R. Malone and Lisa Bero   "Chasing the Dollar: Why Scientists Should Decline Tobacco Industry Funding," *Journal of Epidemiology and Community Health*, 2003.

Monique Muggli et al.

"The Smoke You Don't See: Uncovering Tobacco Industry Scientific Strategies Aimed Against Environmental Tobacco Smoke Policies," *American Journal of Public Health*, 2001.

Ed Nelson

"The Miseries of Passive Smoking," *Human & Experimental Toxicology*, 2001.

Elisa Ong and Stanton Glantz

"Constructing 'Sound Science' and 'Good Epidemiology': Tobacco, Lawyers, and Public Relations Firms," *American Journal of Public Health*, 2001.

Linda Rosenstock and Lore Jackson Lee

"Attacks on Science: The Risks to Evidence-Based Policy," *American Journal of Public Health*, 2002.

Suzaynn Schick and Stanton Glantz

"Philip Morris Toxicological Experiments with Fresh Sidestream Smoke: More Toxic than Mainstream Smoke," *Tobacco Control*, 2005.

Sara Schroter et al.

"Does the Type of Competing Interest Statement Affect Readers' Perceptions of the Credibility of Research? Randomised Trial," *BMJ*, 2004.

Elizabeth A. Smith

"'It's Interesting How Few People Die from Smoking': Tobacco Industry Efforts to Minimize Risk and Discredit Health Promotion," *European Journal of Public Health*, 2007.

Richard Smith "Conflicts of Interest: How Money Clouds Objectivity," *Journal of the Royal Society of Medicine*, 2006.

Richard Smith "Making Progress with Competing Interests," *BMJ*, 2002.

Michael Thun "More Misleading Science from the Tobacco Industry," *BMJ*, 2003.

E. Tong and Stanton Glantz "ARTIST (Asian Regional Tobacco Industry Scientist Team): Philip Morris' Attempt to Exert a Scientific and Regulatory Agenda on Asia," *Tobacco Control*, 2004

Index